MASTERMIND® MATHEMATICS
Logic, Strategies, and Proofs

Mathew Mitchell

KEY CURRICULUM PRESS
Innovators in Mathematics Education

Editor	Dan Bennett
Editorial Assistant	James A. Browne
Production Editor	Jason Luz
Production Manager	Diana Jean Parks
Copyeditor	Joseph Siegel
Design Coordinator	Diana Krevsky
Cover Design	Ellen Silva
Interior Design, Art, and Composition	Joe Spooner
Cover Photo	Elizabeth Fenwick
Publisher	Steven Rasmussen
Editorial Director	John Bergez

Key Curriculum Press
1150 65th Street
Emeryville, CA 94608
510-595-7000

editorial@keypress.com
http://www.keypress.com

MASTERMIND® is a registered trademark of Pressman Toy Corporation, New York, NY 10010, © 1981 under agreement with Invicta Plastics Limited UK MEMO B.L.A. Made in the U.S.A.

Printed in the United States of America

10 9 8 7 6 5 4 3 2   03 02 01 00 99

ISBN 1-55953-319-6

To my parents, Beth and Fred Mitchell, who taught me to enjoy and learn from games of strategy and logic; to my wife, Susan Prion, with whom I am always learning that "work" and "play" are opposite sides of the same coin; and to my editors, Dan Bennett and James Browne, who have helped to make this a much better book.

Contents

INTRODUCTION

For the Teacher

Problem solving takes many forms. Many educators and policymakers are highly concerned with students acquiring critical problem-solving skills. Unfortunately there is little agreement on what these skills are and how they should be taught. Nonetheless, a rich background of research indicates that most people have pronounced difficulties thinking deductively and using fundamental problem-solving strategies. This book looks at one possible path for learning specific deductive thinking and problem-solving skills. The instructional approach chosen for this book is to use a simple yet instructionally rich game that enhances learning by combining key motivational and cognitive factors.

Students young and old are fascinated by simple yet challenging games. The idea of using games or game-like elements for instruction is not new to mathematics teachers. Game-like learning environments allow students to feel that they are simply having fun while they are simultaneously learning serious mathematical skills. For example, many teachers use "brainteasers" or "logic puzzles" to start off a class period. Other teachers have adapted such games as "Jeopardy" or "Wheel of Fortune" to create contest settings that help students learn important mathematical terms or theorems.

Why are games motivational? Games are perceived by students as environments with clear rules in which they can have fun by tackling progressively challenging situations. Games allow students to naturally develop their skills by providing immediate and timely feedback for their actions. And games keep students "hooked" by embedding curiosity into their structure. One only has to think about the nature of many video games to see a structure that has clear rules, progressive challenges (i.e., the different levels of many video games), clear and immediate feedback, and curiosity elements built into the game environment. MASTERMIND is a classic game that includes all of these key elements of effective game environments.

Why do games like MASTERMIND seem so well adapted to teaching higher-level thinking skills? All too often students associate mathematics with learning a set of algorithms. However, students work incredibly hard to be skilled at a game. MASTERMIND is based on hypothesis testing and deductive reasoning. Thus, if students learn to play MASTERMIND with appropriate instruction, they quickly see the usefulness of such skills as abstraction, deductive reasoning, making a chart, eliminating possibilities, using pattern-searching strategies, proof by contradiction, and writing mathematical proofs. These are all skills that are central to good mathematical thinking and students need to learn and practice them.

This curriculum is easily suited to a constructivist classroom where a teacher uses artful dialogue and discussion to help students discover the material to be learned, rather than simply "telling" it. On the other hand, teachers who are more comfortable within a traditional classroom setting will also be able to use the materials with great benefit to their students. The eight main benefits for students of *MASTERMIND Mathematics* are:

1. Games help students become more **motivated learners**.
2. Practice in abstraction helps students become better **abstract thinkers**.
3. Strategies help students become better **problem solvers**.
4. Proofs help students become better **communicators**.
5. The cognitive modeling provided in this book helps students become better **metacognitive thinkers**.
6. Challenges help students become **expert** players/thinkers.
7. Adaptability helps teachers have a **choice** in how they use the instructional materials.
8. Connections help teachers **build bridges** between MASTERMIND and mathematics.

How to Use This Book

MASTERMIND Mathematics is a supplementary curriculum that takes from 3 to 12 weeks to implement. The materials are highly adaptable so that they may be used in a variety of ways. In this section, the following issues are discussed:

◆ Using *MASTERMIND Mathematics* as a full-time curriculum
◆ Using the curriculum on a part-time, supplementary basis
◆ Using the curriculum for enrichment purposes
◆ Curriculum alternatives based on how many MASTERMIND gameboards a teacher has
◆ Photocopying and presentation alternatives
◆ Creating your own game situations
◆ The MASTERMIND Olympics

The Three-Week Curriculum

One way to use the book is to devote a part of the semester full-time to *MASTERMIND Mathematics*. For example, some geometry teachers take 2 to 4 weeks during the school year to teach students about deductive thinking. In a similar fashion, *MASTERMIND Mathematics* would help your students get an intuitive jump-start on how to think deductively, to consciously use key problem-solving skills, and to write mathematical proofs. You could use Chapters 1 through 3 in the first week, Chapters 4 through 6 in the second week, and Chapters 7 and 8 in the third week. You could then use Chapter 9 as a source of very challenging problems for students who are ready to take them on. You may want to take more than three weeks based on the previous skills and general learning pace of your students. However you implement the full curriculum, *MASTERMIND Mathematics* can establish a powerful foundation in mathematical thinking.

The Part-Time Curriculum

You can also use *MASTERMIND Mathematics* as a part-time, supplementary curriculum. Since the games are naturally intriguing to students, you might choose to use the problem games as brainteasers or as a warm-up to begin each class. During a 10-minute period, students could profitably work on a problem supported with a follow-up discussion led by you or by student demonstrations. To make sure that students actually increase their skills in a timely fashion, give some games as homework so students don't work on the problems *only* in the first 10 minutes of class. In this way, *MASTERMIND Mathematics* could be covered in one-half to two-thirds of a semester. The one caveat with this approach is that there will be points where you will need some relatively short lecture time to go over the key skills in the book. Thus, while the 10-minute warm-up approach will work on many days, it will not work as the *only* way to implement the curriculum.

The Enrichment Curriculum

MASTERMIND Mathematics can be used as special homework or in-class activities for students needing enrichment activities within the regular classroom. It can also be a useful resource in a mathematics club. Most, if not all, of the activities in the book lend themselves to mathematical discussion and mathematical communication. Students often convince each other of solutions or strategies or proofs more effectively than teachers. If you use the curriculum for enrichment or for a math club, it is important that students have opportunities to "talk it out."

Alternatives to Using the Physical MASTERMIND Gameboard

MASTERMIND Mathematics works on the assumption that you are using the book in conjunction with the physical game. This is the advised way of proceeding through the book. The physical gameboard is not needed for the entire curriculum, however. Students can, at any point, play the games in the book using only paper-and-pencil. However, for many learners the use of the gameboard itself is very important in the early stages of the curriculum. If you don't have access to the gameboard at all, you can simulate the gameboard structure with colored circles. Though this would take a little time to create, low-cost gameboards made out of cardboard or colored paper can work well.

One of the keys to this curriculum is letting students take the time necessary to think through their game moves. Both the physical gameboard and the abstract paper-and-pencil version of the game do this. It is possible to download or play computerized versions of the game from the World Wide Web. This can be a tantalizing option for many teachers. If there are sufficient computers, it allows each student to play the game (instead of one student playing and another being the codemaker). Yet in most educational settings this is not a good option. Too many students use the computerized versions in ways that are not conducive to conversation or good logical thinking. While exceptions surely exist, be aware that using a computerized version of the game may not be as helpful as having two people play and discuss the game.

Many teachers will find themselves between the two extremes of having a gameboard for every student and having none at all. The ideal is to have one gameboard for every two students since two people are normally playing the game. However, reasonable alternatives exist. One option is to have three students at each gameboard. In this setup two students try to solve the code together. In some ways this can be better than the two-person setup as the two codebreakers often share fruitful conversations with one another about strategies. Another option is to have only a few students be codemakers (e.g., 4 in a classroom of 36). The codemaker writes the Mastercode on a piece of paper (instead of in the specific section set aside for this on the playing board). This Mastercode serves as the same Mastercode for four groups of two students trying to solve the code. The codemaker, then, is always responding to the new moves on four different boards. Using the same Mastercode for all four boards makes this a tenable situation since students tend not to make moves quickly, but instead think about their next moves for a while. In short, this leads to a situation with 1 codemaker for 8 playing students. You are left free to observe, comment, and coach as students try to solve the problems.

Photocopying and Presentation Alternatives

With the exception of this introduction for teachers, *MASTERMIND Mathematics* is written for student readers. In the best case, all students would be able to use the physical game and all students would have a copy of the book *MASTERMIND Mathematics*. Nonetheless, you can easily reproduce portions of *MASTERMIND Mathematics* for an overhead projector or to distribute to students.

Many pages contain two or three game situations. Depending on the capabilities of the class and the specific difficulties of the problem, one page will often be enough to serve as problems, lead-ins for discussion, and elaboration for an entire class period. If you want to use the games for 10-minute warm-ups, cut the copies and distribute one game at a time.

The way *MASTERMIND Mathematics* is organized allows you to use either direct instruction or a more constructivist approach to instruction. Some may want to provide direct instruction to students about the concept of the "Overload Method" before engaging in any of the MASTERMIND problems which take advantage of that method. Other teachers may want to use a more constructivist approach in which the first one or two games in the section serve as the basis for discovering how a strategy like the "Overload Method" can be extremely useful in solving game situations. Either approach can be used easily in the *MASTERMIND Mathematics* curriculum.

However you choose to use *MASTERMIND Mathematics*, a key component of this approach to learning is that students profit by being mathematical communicators. This is explicitly addressed in the two chapters on mathematical proofs—that is, how do you convince another person in mathematical terms? But throughout the book students learn better when they have the opportunity to talk about their approaches to solving a game and their particular thinking about moves and strategies. To help you facilitate this approach, the book includes many vignettes of how a fictional MASTERMIND player might think aloud about a particular game or game setting. You may want to use these monologues as models of how to think about specific game situations. Provide copies of these to students, or paraphrase them orally yourself.

In short, *MASTERMIND Mathematics* is a powerful, highly flexible, and adaptable approach to learning fundamental mathematical thinking skills. Enjoy and have fun increasing the thinking skills of your students.

Creating Your Own Game Situations

While numerous game situations have been provided in this book, you may want to provide additional games for the entire class, or for some students, to work on. While it is difficult to create your own game scenarios from scratch (you need to be very careful with logical inconsistencies), it is fairly simple to create game situations which are isomorphic to the ones in the book. By isomorphic, I mean games that have the same internal structure but which, on the surface, look very different. Thus, if Game 5 (for example) is a difficulty level that you want students to practice more before going on to other games, creating your own isomorphic games is quite useful. Below I give two separate algorithms for making these isomorphic changes. Each of the algorithms assumes that you are working with a 5-move game. Depending on the actual number of moves in a game, you may have to adapt the move section of the algorithm slightly. However, the color section of the algorithms will always work no matter how many moves are used in a particular game situation.

CHANGE ALGORITHM #1		CHANGE ALGORITHM #2	
Colors	Moves	Colors	Moves
Y→R	Move 1 → Move 2	Y→B	Move 1 → Move 4
B→G	Move 2 → Move 4	B→W	Move 2 → Move 1
O→W	Move 3 → Move 5	O→G	Move 3 → Move 2
W→Y	Move 4 → Move 3	W→R	Move 4 → Move 5
G→O	Move 5 → Move 1	G→Y	Move 5 → Move 3
R→B		R→O	

The key to using the algorithm is to first complete all the color changes and then all the changes in the order of the moves, or vice versa. Don't mix up color and move changes simultaneously. Clearly you can also make up your own isomorphic algorithms so that you can create more than two additional isomorphic games for every MASTERMIND game presented in the book.

The MASTERMIND Olympics

The last chapter challenges students with some particularly difficult problems. Not all teachers will want to use these problems in class. Some may want to assign them for extra credit. However, I've found that there are always some students who would like to tackle more challenging and mind-stretching games. These games should provide sufficient challenge for those students!

If you choose to use some or all of the Olympic games in class, you should be aware that it may take one or more class periods to solve a single game and another class period to come up with a satisfactory proof of the Mastercode. It is unlikely that many teachers will be able to take this much time for each of these Olympic games in the classroom. However, students can attempt to do these games as homework. The solutions, or partial solutions, to the Olympic games could then be discussed in class the following day. Another strategy would be to work on one of these problems for 10 minutes a day. Over a school week one problem could be solved.

There are many different pedagogical uses for the MASTERMIND Olympics. Use them in class if you have the time and inclination. If you don't, remember that there will likely be students who would truly enjoy taking on these final exciting MASTERMIND games.

Mathematics and Games

The Core of Mathematics

The purpose of this book is to introduce you to the core of mathematical thinking. Mathematics is not about becoming the quickest student, nor is it simply about numbers or about memorizing the most famous theorems from past centuries. Mathematics is about the process of challenge and discovery. This book is intended to help you develop your problem-solving abilities.

During the course of this book we will be developing our skills at playing the game of MASTERMIND. There will be plenty of fun involved, but also a good dose of hard work. This book does not expect any specific level of ability from you. However, you do need to bring a *desire* to be a better problem solver. If you bring that desire, then by the end of this book you will experience significant growth in your abilities for logical thinking and problem solving.

In addition, by the end of this book you may also have a sense of how mathematics is an art form. The potter works with forming clay, the mathematician works with understanding patterns and in forming logical systems. Just as artists often talk about excellence and elegance in artwork, so do mathematicians speak of "math works." To be a good mathematician often requires you to be creative in your perception and willing to take chances. The artist is a master of aesthetic communication; the mathematician likewise is a master of communicating analytical thinking. In short, mathematics, like art, requires precise skills, creative thought, and the ability to communicate effectively.

Deductive Logic

Much mathematical thinking involves deductive logic. What exactly is the nature of deductive thought? That's a question we'll explore in the process of working through this book. For now, let us take a quick look at how deductive thought works. In essence this type of thinking allows us to start off with a few statements that we accept as true (imagine being a detective here starting with a few pieces of evidence) and then to apply those statements and the rules of logic to establish the truth of other, new statements. Just as a detective may use a few facts combined with impeccable logic to conclude something new, mathematicians are constantly creating new truths.

A familiar mathematical example may help. In ancient Greece mathematicians developed geometry as a set of logically proven statements. Mathematicians start off by accepting some statements as true even though they are not proven. These statements tend to be quite simple–concepts that everyone would easily accept. For example, look at the diagram below.

In this situation we have two straight lines which cross one another. One statement that people easily accept is that all straight angles are equal (a straight angle is equal to 180 degrees). If we accept such a statement, then it is easy to see that $\angle a + \angle b = \angle b + \angle c$ since both sides of the equation are derived from straight lines and thus comprise straight angles. Using algebra we can further deduce that $\angle a = \angle c$ because we can subtract $\angle b$ from both sides of the equation. These two angles are conventionally referred to as vertical angles since they are opposite one another when two lines, or line segments, intersect. In summary, by starting with a statement that everyone can accept ("all straight angles are equal") and using our powers of deduction along with some basic algebra, we have created a new statement that we know has to be true: "vertical angles are equal."

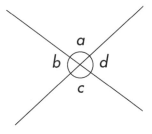

The ancient Greeks started this process of using deductive logic to create new statements and findings. This tradition was preserved by Arab mathematicians after the decline of the ancient Greek empire. Today this same thinking "engine" drives much of mathematical activity throughout the world.

Problem-Solving Skills

A second key component of mathematical thinking is the development of problem-solving skills. These skills can help you to make significant progress on a problem. There are many different problem-solving skills that are useful to mathematical thinking. In this book we explore *seven* specific problem-solving strategies, but there exist many more.

Let's look at an example. Pretend that you need to organize a surprise birthday party for your best friend. You want to invite about 30 people. To make such a birthday party successful involves many preparations: getting permission of your parents to use the house, planning for food, planning when the guests arrive, planning how the birthday person will get to the party so that they are surprised, letting the neighbors know there will be a party going on, and so on. The way I have just described the problem makes it clear that the big problem—organizing a surprise birthday party—is probably more effectively solved by creating a series of subgoals: planning for food, inviting the guests, and so on. Creating subgoals is a problem-solving strategy. You can see that creating subgoals, in and of itself, will not solve the problem. However, creating subgoals does help to make the final problem easier by creating a series of smaller, more easily solvable problems.

Problem solving is a human activity that we engage in all the time. One of the purposes of this book is to provide you with some specific skills in problem solving that will help you in mathematics and possibly in your everyday life!

Games and Learning Mathematics

The way mathematical thinking proceeds is much like a game. To begin, each game we play has rules. Mathematics has rules such as the initial statements that we accept as true and the general rules of deductive logic. Players of games are free to choose actions as long as they stay within the bounds of the rules of the game. Mathematicians are also free to choose many different types of actions as long as they stay within the logical rules.

For example, the game of basketball has rules, and the players move within the game as effectively and creatively as they can. Mathematicians are the same. One purpose of this book is to uncover some of the real "rules" of mathematical thought. Another purpose of the book is to demonstrate how we can all learn to play advantageously within the rules of mathematics.

Why use the game of MASTERMIND to learn skills for mathematical thinking such as deductive reasoning and problem-solving skills? First, MASTERMIND is a game that always involves a problem to be solved. The problem is a secret code that you are trying to uncover. Second, although there are many ways to play MASTERMIND, the most effective methods of playing involve the use of deductive reasoning and some specific problem-solving techniques. Third, as with other games, MASTER-MIND is an activity that many people find fascinating and enjoyable. For all of these reasons MASTERMIND serves as a bridge between games and mathematical activity.

Enjoy MASTERMIND. But most of all, enjoy learning the mathematical skills described in this book as you play the game. Mathematics learning in general can have many of the game-like features of MASTERMIND. Good luck!

The Game of MASTERMIND

How to Play the Game

This chapter will describe how to play the game of MASTERMIND: the object of the game, the game contents, and the game rules. You can also learn how to play by reading the instructions that come with the game. Once you've learned how to play, you'll try some initial explorations into strategies for playing MASTERMIND.

As with most games, the best way to learn is to play. Find a partner and play a practice game or two following the rules below. Once you've learned the rules of the game, you will want to continue playing the game to become more expert at it. Many of the skills and strategies you learn about in this book will be easier to understand if you have played the game many times and have developed your own thinking about how to play it well.

Object of the Game

MASTERMIND is played by two people: a player and a codemaker. The object of MASTERMIND for the player is to guess the hidden code, called the Mastercode, which consists of a series of four colored pegs. With each guess you make, you receive feedback from the codemaker on the accuracy of your guess. This feedback narrows down the possibilities for the Mastercode. Through a series of guesses and feedback you attempt to find the Mastercode in the least possible number of guesses.

Game Contents

The game contains a playing board, color pegs, and feedback pegs. The *playing board* contains holes for placing pegs and a shield to hide the Mastercode from the player (see the diagram on the next page). The color pegs are large round-headed pegs that come in six colors. For games made in 1996 or later the six colors are green, red, yellow, blue, white, and orange. And some versions of the game may have more colors or different colors. However, games made before 1996 use black as a color instead of orange. We assume in this book that you are using a game with six colors, including orange. The feedback pegs are small flat-headed pegs used for giving the player feedback on a specific move. Feedback pegs come in two colors: white and red (in some versions of MASTERMIND the feedback pegs are white and black).

Directions

Step 1   Decide which person is to be the codemaker and which is to be the player. Position the board between the two players so that the four shielded holes for the Mastercode face the codemaker.

Step 2   The codemaker secretly places four color pegs in the four nearest holes. The Mastercode is then covered by flipping over the plastic shield to conceal it from the player. The codemaker can use *any* combination of the six colors. For instance, the codemaker can use two or more like-color pegs. The series of color pegs placed by the codemaker becomes the Mastercode.

Step 3   The player places a combination of color pegs in the first row of the holes. The player is trying to duplicate the exact colors and positions of the Mastercode. Of course, with a first move the player is making a guess.

Step 4   The codemaker responds by placing anywhere from zero to four feedback pegs in the feedback peg holes. Feedback pegs are given on the following basis:

♦ A **red** feedback peg indicates one of the color pegs is both the right color and in the right position. This red feedback peg does not tell the player which of the color pegs this feedback is for.

♦ A **white** feedback peg indicates one of the color pegs is the right color but not in the correct position.

♦ No feedback peg indicates a wrong color.

♦ There should be nothing about the *placement* of the feedback pegs to indicate which particular color pegs the feedback pegs are for. It is part of the challenge of the game for the player to figure out which color peg corresponds to which particular feedback peg.

Step 5   The player places another set of color pegs in the second row and the codemaker places the feedback pegs in the second row as appropriate. The pegs played in each row are left as played until the Mastercode is found.

Step 6   The player keeps placing rows of color pegs and getting feedback from the codemaker until the Mastercode is found. At this point the codemaker places 4 red feedback pegs and reveals the Mastercode (with trumpets sounding in the background).

Step 7   Once the Mastercode is found, the players switch roles and begin a new game.

Tip: People have more difficulty understanding the response when 2 pegs of the same color appear in the Mastercode or in the player's guess or in both. In this situation the basic principle is that one feedback peg corresponds to one *and only one* color peg. If the player's guess uses multiple pegs of the same color and if one of those color placements is the correct color in the correct position, then a red feedback peg should be given. Consider the game situation diagrammed below:

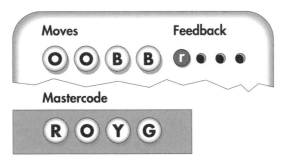

The player used two oranges in the move shown. There is only one orange in the Mastercode. However, since one of the player's oranges was the correct color in the correct position, the feedback is one red feedback peg. However, in the second example game situation given below the situation is different:

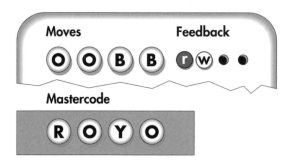

In this second situation one of the player's oranges is still a correct color in a correct position, but now we would consider their second orange to also be a correct color (since there are now two oranges in the Mastercode) but in the wrong position. This means the codemaker would give feedback of one red and one white feedback peg.

For more on how to play MASTERMIND, see the instructions that come with the game.

MASTERMIND Playing Strategies

We encourage you to play MASTERMIND in a playful and mindful manner. Being mindful implies that you think about and reflect upon your actions. The three initial steps suggested below may help jump-start your mindful thinking about MASTER-MIND strategies.

Step 1: Play and Play

Find a willing partner to play the game of MASTERMIND a number of times. You need to play often enough that you feel comfortable with the rules of the game and the game's objectives. There is no need to try to become a master player at this point. That will come about quite naturally by working your way through the chapters in this book. Just become familiar and comfortable with the game. When you reach that point where you do feel at ease with both the rules and objectives of the game, come back to this book and start on Step 2.

Step 2: Strategic Moves

At this point begin to notice if there are "better" strategic moves you can make while playing MASTERMIND. Experiment for a few games. Come up with your own conclusions and strategies.

It may be helpful for you to consider some of the following questions when developing your own strategies.

1. Are there better or worse ways of making a first move?
2. Do you think starting with four different colors is better than starting with four pegs of the same color?
3. How many different colors would you use to start off a game?
4. What about second moves?
5. What kind of response would you like to get back from the codemaker?
6. Do you think three white feedback pegs gives you a lot more information than no feedback pegs at all?
7. Is it always better to get at least one feedback peg (white or red) rather than no feedback pegs at all?
8. Is it ever a good strategy to include in your guess colors that you know are not part of the code?

These are the sort of questions that often help a person to become more conscious about how they are playing the game. Becoming increasingly conscious of how one's thinking process works is at the heart of mathematics. Please feel free to jot down other questions or make notes on what you feel to be the "answers" to the above questions.

Step 3: Let the Games Begin!

Now, instead of your being the "player" we will change the conditions slightly. You will be given an actual series of moves that another player made when trying to solve a Mastercode. Arrange your playing board to exactly match the game diagrams given on the following pages. Use the following key to know how the symbols are represented in this book.

Color Pegs
W = White
R = Red
G = Green
O = Orange
Y = Yellow
B = Blue

Feedback Pegs
w = white
r = red

Given the steps the player had made, see if you can figure out the Mastercode. If you get stuck, remain stuck for a while and continue to try solving the problem. You might want to take a short break and return to the problem. At any rate, write down which colors and/or positions you know *for sure* based on the evidence given. When you can't figure out any more information, then you can refer to the hints that are provided at the end of the chapter. (Note: Three sequential levels of hints are given. Look at only one level of hint at a time.) To check to see if your deduced answer for the Mastercode is correct, refer to the answer key, which is also provided at the end of this chapter.

MASTERMIND GAME 1
6 COLORS, 4 POSITIONS

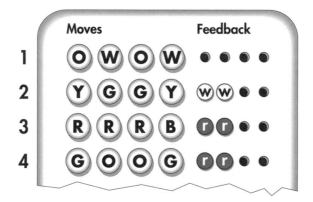

MASTERMIND GAME 2
6 COLORS, 4 POSITIONS

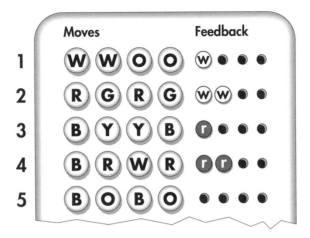

MASTERMIND GAME 3
6 COLORS, 4 POSITIONS

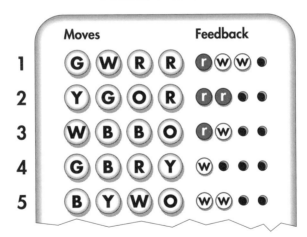

How did you find these first few game situations? Whether you found them easy or difficult does not matter so much at this point. What *is* important is that you stay with a problem until you gain a better understanding of its structure. This demands some perseverance but it also brings up two key rules for using the book effectively:

Rule 1 Move at your own rate.

Rule 2 Move with understanding.

Mathematics is not like some other subjects where if worse comes to worse you can "fake it." This discipline moves by understanding–not by opinions or creative writing. Don't worry about "getting it right." Instead, enjoy exploring each problem. Take the time necessary to see the whole structure of the game situation. Don't get caught up in the impulse for quickness simply because some people associate being quick with being smart. There are many smart people in the world who became that way by taking the time necessary to thoroughly understand a problem. That quality will get you much further than trying to be quick. Go for depth, not flash. Enjoy.

LEVEL-ONE HINTS

Game 1 Look at Move 1. What does it tell you?

Game 2 Look at Move 5. What does it tell you?

Game 3 This is much harder–but can you figure out anything from Move 1? Look at the colors played and the feedback pegs given. (From Move 1 you can tell that Red has to be one of the colors.)

LEVEL-TWO HINTS

Game 1 Given what you already know about the colors in Move 1, what can you deduce from Move 4?

Game 2 Given what you know now about the colors in Move 5, what more can you deduce from Moves 1 and 3?

Game 3 Given what you know about at least one color in Move 1 and other possible colors in Move 1, what can you deduce from Move 4?

LEVEL-THREE HINTS

Game 1 To figure out the rest of the Mastercode, you'll have to work out the possible positions of the colors you found so far. Then look at what other colors could possibly go in the final two vacant positions.

Game 2 Move 4 contains the last essential bits of information–both in terms of color and positioning.

Game 3 Moves 1 and 2 give you lots of additional information about the colors. You will then have to work out the positions on your own.

ANSWERS

Game 1   G R R G

Game 2   G Y W R

Game 3   W R O R

CHAPTER 3

Foundation Strategies

To play MASTERMIND well it helps to have some key strategies up your sleeve. In truth there are probably many different effective strategies for helping you solve MASTERMIND games. In this chapter, however, we will focus on four foundation strategies. In the next chapter we'll begin to explore other sorts of strategies–some of which you may have already found.

The strategies introduced in this chapter are problem-solving strategies that you can use in many different realms of life. You may recognize these as strategies you've used to solve mathematical problems. The strategies we'll look at are:

- ◆ Establish subgoals
- ◆ Make a chart
- ◆ Use deductive thinking
- ◆ Eliminate possibilities

Establish Subgoals

Many beginning players of MASTERMIND try to figure out both the colors and their positions in the Mastercode at the same time. Generally speaking this is not a good idea. The big goal, of course, is to find the Mastercode. However, by establishing some useful subgoals you can break the problem into smaller problems which are easier to handle.

In a MASTERMIND game there are 6 colors and 4 positions. That means there are 6^4 (or 1,296) different combinations of codes that the codemaker could create. However, let's say that you are not interested in positions, but only in the subgoal of finding the correct colors. In that case there are only 126 different groups of colors possible.* So, by focusing on colors you can reduce the difficulty of the problem by almost 90%. Of course once you have the colors, you then need to find the positions too. But, once you have the colors, there are only 24 different codes that could be made from a specific set of colors when working with 4 positions. Most people would look forward to breaking down a complex problem (i.e., one with 1,296 possible answers) into two subgoals for which one has 126 possible answers and the other 24.

In general, it is best for you to find all the correct colors before worrying about the correct positions. When you have all the colors, then you can find the positions more easily. Once in a while you will need to find one or more positions before you can definitely figure out all of the colors. This brings up an important point about strategies: they do not *always* work. They serve as good guidelines, yet you must always use discretion when you find a specific strategy is not serving you well in a specific game.

Make a Chart

People often use charts to make information fit into a format that is more easily understood. When playing MASTERMIND it is quite useful to have a diagram or chart which shows you exactly which colors you know for sure are, or are not, in the Mastercode.

The general form of a useful chart for solving MASTERMIND is shown below.

On the left-hand side (under the check mark) you list those colors you know are correct (henceforth referred to as the *correct* column). On the right-hand side (under the "x") you list those colors you know are incorrect. For example, after three moves

---

*The formula for finding the number of combinations in which there is replacement (i.e., the same color can be used over and over again) but order (or position) is unimportant is given by: $(M + n - 1)! / (n! \cdot M - 1!)$. M is the number of colors (6), n is how many colors you are selecting (4), so you get: $(6 + 4 - 1)! / (4! \cdot 5!) = 9! / 4! \cdot 5! = 9 \cdot 8 \cdot 7 \cdot 6 / 4 \cdot 3 \cdot 2 \cdot 1 = 9 \cdot 7 \cdot 2 = 126$. You may want to find a probability book to learn more about this formula, then see if you can figure out how it applies to this and other MASTERMIND possibilities.

you might be able to deduce the following:

◆ Red and Orange are incorrect colors.
◆ Green and White are correct colors.
◆ Yellow and Blue cannot be determined *for sure* yet.

Your chart would then look like this:

✔	✗
G	R
W	O

It is important to put down *only* those colors you are absolutely sure about. Often you will have hunches or suspicions about certain colors. That's fine, but don't put them into your chart until you are positive about their status.

One of the biggest advantages of drawing a diagram is that it greatly reduces *cognitive overload*. This is a fancy way of saying that when we have to store too much information in our short-term memory, then some of the information gets lost. Given that everyone has a limited range of attention, it is often wise to jot down relatively mundane information (such as colors) and use your brain power for figuring out the code. The more basic information your brain tries to store in

Short-term memory   Cognitive overload

short-term memory, the harder it is for you to also think strategically. This means that the more difficult a problem is, the more useful a chart is.

We also need to decide on a convention for the situation in which we discover more than one bit of information about the same color. First, we could find out that there is more than one correct peg representing White (e.g., there are two or three Whites in the code). Second, we could find out that the color has one place in the Mastercode but that it definitely does not have two places in the code. How would we represent such situations? Our first suggestion is that you represent the second use of a color with the prefix of 2. Let's look at the chart below:

✔	✗
W	R
2W	G

This chart tells us that the Mastercode *must* include two whites (because we have one white, W, and a second white, 2W, in the correct column).

Our second suggestion is that you think of the correct column as meaning "at least" (as in "at least two Whites are in the Mastercode"). To indicate "exactly" you could circle a color in the correct column. Let's look at the chart below:

✔	✗
W	R
2W	G
(Y)	

From this chart we know there is one and only one Yellow in the Mastercode.

Deductive Logic

Deductive reasoning is a very powerful tool. Deduction is the process of finding the logical implications of what we already know (or assume) to be true. For example, let's say we accept the following statements as true:

1. All people are mortal.
2. Alice Walker is a person.

From these assumptions we can deduce that:

Alice Walker is mortal.

What we accepted as true has logically led us to certain conclusions. Deductive reasoning is often referred to as IF-THEN thinking because it proceeds by stating IF _____ is true, THEN _____ must necessarily be true. For example, IF it's true that Alice Walker is a person, THEN it's necessarily true that Alice Walker is mortal.

In playing MASTERMIND, each move with its accompanying feedback serves as the IF-part of a deductive statement. Let's look at an example.

MASTERMIND GAME 4
6 COLORS, 4 POSITIONS

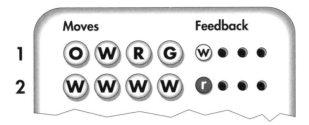

From the above plays we can deduce:

♦ White is a correct color (from Move 2)
♦ Orange, Red, and Green are incorrect.

Let's now take a look at how someone might *deductively* think aloud about this game situation.

MASTERMIND REASONING FOR GAME 4

Okay, from Move 2 I know White must be correct because there is one feedback peg and only one color (four times) for the whole move. Great. Then Move 1 shows me that the one feedback peg must represent the White color. Therefore the other colors must be incorrect since there is only one feedback peg. Thus Orange, Red, and Green are not in the code.

A more formal way to express the same line of thinking would be: IF white is a correct color AND IF only one color in Move 1 is correct, THEN orange, green, and red are necessarily incorrect.

Deductive reasoning can always be used in conjunction with other problem-solving skills. Thus deductive reasoning can also be used with the subgoals and make-a-chart strategies. Deductive thinking is an incredibly powerful tool. It always works by starting from some known truths or assumptions (the IF part of a statement) and then finding out what we can conclude *for sure* based on our set of truths or assumptions. This type of thinking proves to be quite powerful in both mathematics and in playing MASTERMIND.

Eliminate Possibilities

This strategy is really a substrategy of deductive reasoning. It involves a "mindset" which is often of use in solving complex problems. The straightforward approach to solving a MASTERMIND problem would be to find which colors and positions are in the Mastercode. Many times this general approach will work. Nonetheless, remember that when we eliminate a possibility we have also gained a lot of information. Consider a move using four different colors that gets no feedback pegs. While it may seem bad luck to guess four colors "wrong," you'll soon recognize the "no feedback" move as incredibly useful. After all, now you have eliminated four colors *for sure* from the Mastercode! That means that at most two colors (if you are playing a six-color game) make up the Mastercode. Likewise the ability to eliminate a particular position as the correct one for a specific color in the Mastercode can be very useful. Perhaps Sir Arthur Conan Doyle's detective character Sherlock Holmes put it best when he said, "When you have eliminated the impossible, whatever remains, however improbable, must be the truth."

Let's look at an example where we need to use deductive reasoning and the strategy of eliminating specific possibilities to find out whether a color is used more than once.

MASTERMIND GAME 5
6 COLORS, 4 POSITIONS

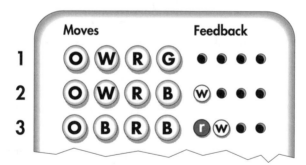

MASTERMIND REASONING FOR GAME 5

I know, from Move 1, that Orange, White, Red, and Green are all incorrect colors. I've eliminated them from the Mastercode. If those four colors are incorrect, that means that in Move 2 Blue must be the correct color. Okay, great. Again, if I know Orange and Red are incorrect, then from Move 3 I additionally know that there must be at least two Blues in the Mastercode.

So this is what I know so far:

✔	✗
B	O
2B	W
	R
	G

I can't tell anything else for sure about the colors at this point. On the other hand I can figure out something about the positions. I can eliminate the possibility of Blue going in Position 4 by Move 2. Therefore I know one Blue needs to go in Position 2 by Move 3. So the second Blue must go in either Position 1 or 3.

Exceptions to the Rule

Once in a while you will be in a game in which you can't follow a specific strategy strictly. For example, we stated earlier that it is generally useful to first figure out what the correct colors are and then worry about figuring out the positions. But this is not always good advice. Consider the game given below.

MASTERMIND GAME 6
6 COLORS, 4 POSITIONS

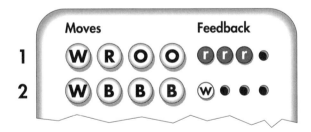

In the case of this game, using position information and deductive reasoning will help you greatly–even before you have determined all the colors. Let's look at how someone might reason this game out.

MASTERMIND REASONING FOR GAME 6

Hmm, I know from Move 1 that whatever colors are correct they are also all in the right positions. But Move 2 tells me that whatever color is correct is *not* in

---

the right position. Since White is in exactly the same position in both moves—and in each case there is only one White—then White can't be correct.

Now I know from Move 1 that Red and two Oranges must be correct. Furthermore I know that Red goes in Position 2 and the Oranges go in Positions 3 and 4. In Move 2 Blue must be correct since White has been eliminated. Since three positions in the Mastercode are already known, then the Blue color has to go in Position 1. That's it. So the code is: Blue, Red, Orange, Orange.

To help develop your beginning MASTERMIND foundation strategies, try out the following three game situations. All you want to do with Games 7, 8, and 9 is to make a chart that illustrates all of the information you can glean about correct and incorrect colors from the given moves. Don't try to figure out the complete Mastercode—it may not be possible with the information you are given in these problems.

MASTERMIND GAME 7
6 COLORS, 4 POSITIONS

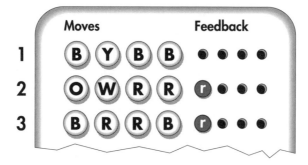

Challenge: Make a chart of the colors you know are (or are not) in the Mastercode.

MASTERMIND GAME 8
6 COLORS, 4 POSITIONS

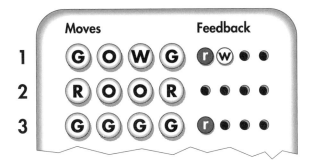

Challenge: Make a chart of the colors you know are (or are not) in the Mastercode.

MASTERMIND GAME 9
6 COLORS, 4 POSITIONS

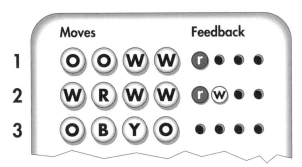

Challenge: Make a chart of the colors you know are (or are not) in the Mastercode.

Using foundation strategies such as subgoals, making a chart, using deductive reasoning, and eliminating possibilities can be powerful approaches to solving for a Mastercode. Below you'll find four games to help hone your newfound skills. In these games you not only want to make a chart, but the challenge is to find the complete Mastercode. Good luck!

MASTERMIND GAME 10
6 COLORS, 4 POSITIONS

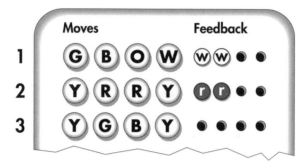

MASTERMIND GAME 11
6 COLORS, 4 POSITIONS

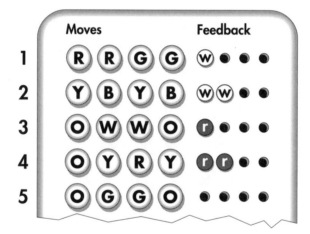

MASTERMIND GAME 12
6 COLORS, 4 POSITIONS

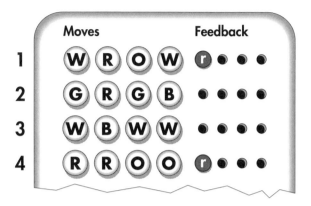

MASTERMIND GAME 13
6 COLORS, 4 POSITIONS

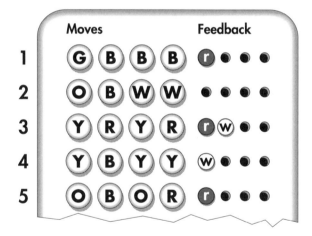

MASTERMIND ANSWERS FOR GAMES 7–13

Game 7 *Challenge: Make a chart.* Here's the chart you can deduce:

✔	✗
(R)	B
G	Y
2G	O
(3G)	W

Notice that you can deduce that there are Greens in the Mastercode due to the elimination of the other colors. This is a very nice way to uncover information even though a Green peg was never played!

Game 8 *Challenge: Make a chart.* Here's the chart you can deduce:

✔	✗
(G)	R
W	O

Game 9 *Challenge: Make a chart.* Here's the chart you can deduce:

✔	✗
(W)	O
R	B
	Y

LEVEL-ONE HINTS

Note: For all of the games it is best to make a chart!

Game 10   What colors can you eliminate based on Move 3?

Game 11   Look at Move 5.

Game 12   From Moves 2 and 3 what colors are incorrect?

Game 13   Move 2 gives you lots of information! Use it in conjunction with Moves 1, 4, and 5.

LEVEL-TWO HINTS

Game 10   What colors do Moves 1 and 2 tell you are in the Mastercode?

Game 11   What colors do you know from Moves 1, 3, and 4?

Game 12   By Moves 1 and 4, what color is correct? Can that color be used more than once?

Game 13   One color has to be used more than once. What is the only color that can be?

LEVEL-THREE HINTS

Game 10   Move 2 tells you two positions. Move 1 gives information for other positions.

Game 11   Find the color that can be figured out in Move 2.

Game 12   What color is missing that must take up the remaining positions?

Game 13   What does Move 4 tell you about the only correct position the correct color can have in that move?

ANSWERS

Game 10 W R R O

Game 11 B W R Y

Game 12 Y Y O Y

Game 13 G Y G R

MASTERMIND Mathematics: Logic, Strategies, and Proofs • ©1999 Key Curriculum Press

Pattern-Searching Strategies

You've begun to see what a powerful problem-solving strategy deductive reasoning can be. The strategies presented in the previous chapter were problem-solving skills that could be used in almost every area of mathematics and in daily life, too! The strategies presented in this chapter are quite specific to the game of MASTERMIND. This is typical in all problem-solving situations: problems often are solved using a combination of *general* problem-solving skills along with problem-solving skills which are *specific* to the area/subject you are studying. Through a combination of general and specific problem-solving skills, people can become master problem solvers.

In MASTERMIND one of the key skills you need is the ability to infer information from patterns—that is, patterns both of colors and of positions. In this chapter we explore two new strategies which both take advantage of deductive reasoning combined with searching for patterns. You can glean a great deal of information from patterns—information that makes it much easier to find the Mastercode.

Consider the following game situation:

Can you tell anything for sure about the Mastercode from this move? Why or why not? Think carefully about your response before reading on.

The Overload Method

In the game situation above you can tell one thing for sure: there *must* be at least one Red in the Mastercode. You can also deduce that there is either an Orange or a White or both in the Mastercode—but at this point you don't know *for sure* any additional colors or positions besides the fact that there is at least one Red in the Mastercode.

The key to this line of thinking is that there are three feedback pegs (whether white or red doesn't matter) for four positions. Thus even if one feedback peg stands for the Orange and a second feedback peg for the White, there would remain one feedback peg left over. Since *both* leftover colors are Red, the last feedback peg must represent a red color. Therefore at least one Red is in the Mastercode.

Consider the following game situation:

Can you tell anything for sure about the Mastercode in this case? Why or why not? Again, think carefully about your response before continuing.

Yes, in fact you can tell there must be at least one Yellow in the Mastercode. The key is that there are two response pegs for four positions. Thus at least one of the feedback pegs would have to stand for one of the yellow colors.

Okay, now that you're warming up the brain cells and getting good at this, consider the following game situation:

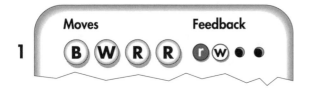

Can you tell anything for sure about the Mastercode in this case? Think hard.

In this situation you could tell, for sure, absolutely nothing about any one color. The key is that there are two responses for four positions. Since there are three different colors used, it is impossible to deduce that any one color has to be in the Mastercode.

The game situations above were examples of implementing a strategy we call the **Overload Method**. This method involves looking for situations in which we can tell at least one color in the Mastercode for sure. We call this approach the Overload Method because it denotes situations in which multiple uses of one color, combined with the number of feedback pegs, have overloaded the game move and force us to deduce that at least one of that color must be in the Mastercode.

Please note two important conditions:

1. We can never have an **overload** situation when all of the colors are different.
2. Even when one color is used more than once, we may not have an **overload** situation.

Row Compare Method

The Overload Method was quite an effective way to spot one specific kind of pattern that can occur during a MASTERMIND game. Let's now look at a second powerful strategy for spotting a specific type of game pattern. Consider the following game situation. Can you tell anything for sure about the Mastercode? Why or why not? Think about your response before continuing.

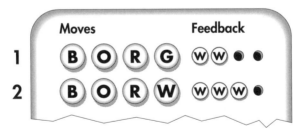

In this game situation you can tell that White is correct and Green is incorrect. The key is that the only difference between the two moves is the Green in Move 1 and the White in Move 2. Both colors are in the fourth position. Note that there was an increase in feedback pegs: from 2 in Move 1 to 3 feedback pegs in Move 2. The *only* way this could happen is if the Green was an incorrect color and the White a correct color. Why? Nothing else has changed. So, if the feedback pegs change and only one color has changed, it must be that one color change that created the feedback change. Thus deductive reasoning tells us that IF two rows differ in the number of feedback pegs and yet differ by only one color, THEN it must be that one changed color that caused the increase (or decrease) in responses.

Now consider the following situation:

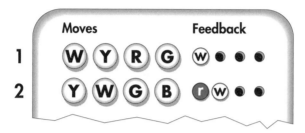

Can you tell anything for sure about the Mastercode? Actually, yes. You can tell there must be a Blue in the Mastercode and not a Red. How do we know? Well, even though the order has changed, the only colors that are different between Move 1 and Move 2 are the Red and the Blue. Since Move 2 has one more feedback peg, it must be because the Blue is correct—which also means that the Red is incorrect.

From the two examples given above, let's look a little more carefully at the Row Compare Method. In order for the strategy to work you need:

1. Two rows where the colors vary only by one color.
2. One of the two rows with one more feedback peg than the other.

For simplicity let's name the row with the fewer responses as MoveLess and the other row as MoveMore. When both of the conditions above occur, it tells you that the different color in MoveLess is *not* in the Mastercode while the different color in MoveMore *is* in the Mastercode.

The Row Compare Method is an extremely powerful tool. Like the Overload Method, it requires you to recognize significant patterns of play. However, the Overload Method only requires you to spot one move that contains the right overload patterns. The Row Compare Method requires spotting two different moves that vary only in one color and one feedback peg. This is not always easy to do. In our examples the moves have been right next to one another (e.g., Move 2 and Move 3) but this need not always be the case. For example, in a real game it may be Move 2 and Move 7 that lend themselves to the Row Compare Method. Also, you may need to do some rearranging (in your mind or on paper) to check that two moves really do meet both conditions of the Row Compare Method. In summary, the Row Compare Method can be much harder to recognize than the Overload Method.

Want a final hint? In a game with many moves, first look for moves that differ by one in their feedback pegs. Then check to see if those moves differ by only one color in their arrangement. This may help simplify the search for a Row Compare situation for you.

Why is Row Compare a strong method? Perhaps the most important reason is that it always allows you to make *two* conclusions. One conclusion is about a color that has to be correct, while the other conclusion is about a color that has to be incorrect. Both types of information are usually equally valuable in figuring out a Mastercode.

Look at the real game situation below and see what you can deduce from the information given.

MASTERMIND GAME 14
6 COLORS, 4 POSITIONS

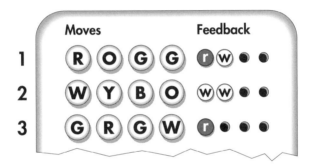

Let's now take a look at how someone might deductively think aloud about this game situation.

MASTERMIND REASONING FOR GAME 14

Hmm, there don't seem to be any Overload situations. Nothing else that I can spot. Maybe the Row Compare strategy would work here. But Moves 1 and 2 are quite different. Can't work there. Moves 2 and 3 are also very different. No help there. Oh, but Moves 1 and 3 are quite similar. Move 1 has two feedback pegs and Move 3 has only one. Good. Move 1 has two Greens and a Red while Move 3 also has two Greens and a Red. So, the only way the two moves differ is that Move 1 has an orange color while Move 3 has a white color. Great, everything we need to do a Row Compare. I can just ignore position information for now. So, since the only thing that changes between the two moves is the Orange and the White, I would need to conclude that the Orange is in, and the White is out. Great, this helps me a lot.

Unfortunately there's not a whole lot more we can deduce from the given information.

To help you develop your beginning MASTERMIND pattern-searching strategies using Row Compare, try out the following three game situations. Keep in mind that you *may not* be able to solve the complete game based on the information given. The challenge is to figure out as much information as possible.

MASTERMIND GAME 15
6 COLORS, 4 POSITIONS

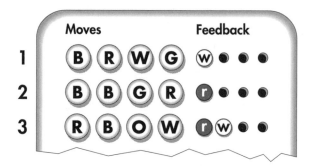

Challenge: Draw a diagram of the colors you know are (or are not) in the Mastercode.

MASTERMIND GAME 16
6 COLORS, 4 POSITIONS

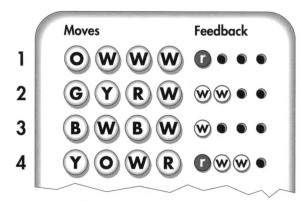

Challenge: Draw a diagram of the colors you know are (or are not) in the Mastercode.

MASTERMIND GAME 17
6 COLORS, 4 POSITIONS

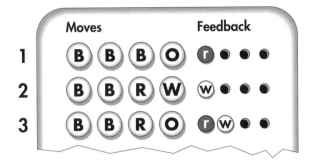

Challenge: Draw a diagram of the colors you know are (or are not) in the Mastercode.

Solve Some Games

Pattern-searching strategies such as the Overload Method and the Row Compare Method can be powerful approaches for solving a Mastercode. Below you'll find two games to help hone your newfound skills. Solving these games may, or may *not*, require the use of either the Overload Method or the Row Compare Method. Game 19 is particularly challenging. Good luck!

MASTERMIND GAME 18
6 COLORS, 4 POSITIONS

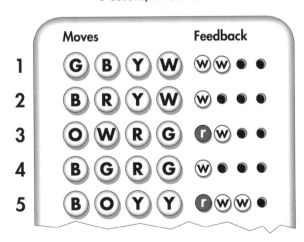

MASTERMIND GAME 19
6 COLORS, 4 POSITIONS

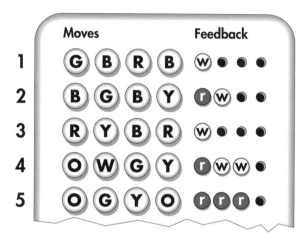

LEVEL-ONE HINTS

Note: For all of the games it is best to draw a diagram!

Game 15   Row Compare Method for Moves 1 and 3 (Orange in, Green out).

Game 16   Row Compare with Moves 2 and 4 (Orange in, Green out).

Game 17   Row Compare with Moves 2 and 3 (Orange in, White out).

Game 18   Use Overload Method with Move 5.

Game 19   Row Compare with Moves 1 and 2.

LEVEL-TWO HINTS

Game 15   Can't tell anything more except that 2 Blues are <u>not</u> in the Mastercode (Move 2).

Game 16   Look at Move 1 and eliminate White.

Game 17   Look at Move 1. Blue is out because we know that Orange is in. What other color needs to be in the Mastercode? Alternatively, you could Row Compare with Moves 1 and 3 (Red in, Blue out).

Game 18   Row Compare with Moves 1 and 2.

Game 19   Move 5 yields to the Overload Method.

LEVEL-THREE HINTS

Game 15   Can't tell anything more.

Game 16   Figure out position for Red after you know position for Orange.

Game 17   Can't figure out the whole game from the information given, but one knows that Orange is in Position 4 and Red is in either Position 1 or 2.

Game 18   For positions, look at Move 4 then Move 3. This will tell you where the Orange must go. In addition, Moves 1 and 4 tell where Green must go.

Game 19   Moves 4 and 5 can be used to deduce where Yellow can't go. Need to already know something about positions.

ANSWERS

Game 15   not solvable

✔	✗
O	G
	2B

Game 16   O B Y R

✔	✗
O	G
Y	W
R	
B	

Game 17   not solvable

✔	✗
O	W
R	B

Game 18   O Y G Y

Game 19   O G Y G

CHAPTER 5

Reduction to the Absurd!

Look at Game 20 and see if you can find the Mastercode. As you may notice after a while, the problem is not very easy. If you find the Mastercode, can you then explain to another person how you reasoned it out? Make sure you take 5 minutes or more to try solving this problem. Make notes of what you are able to figure out and where you get stuck. Good luck!

MASTERMIND GAME 20
6 COLORS, 4 POSITIONS

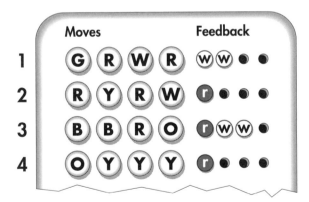

You probably made some headway with Game 20, even if you didn't solve it completely. Let's first look at some of the information we can glean from this game using some MASTERMIND reasoning.

INITIAL MASTERMIND REASONING FOR GAME 20

I first looked at Move 3. Using the Overload Method, I know Blue must be a correct color. I also know from Move 2 that there cannot be two Reds. And I know from Move 4 there cannot be two Yellows. Oh, and there is a Row Compare I can do with Moves 1 and 2! In both moves there are two Reds and one White. However, Move 1 has two feedback pegs and Move 2 has only one. That means that Green must be correct in Move 1 and Yellow must be incorrect in Move 2. That means that in Move 4 the Orange must be a correct color (in the correct position) since Yellow is incorrect. Hmm . . . but now it is hard to deduce anything else for sure. I'm stuck.

At this point we could hazard a guess, use our intuition, or flip a coin to help us decide which is the right combination of colors. That would be unfortunate, though, since a skilled deductive logician could figure this one out for sure! To solve the code requires one more powerful strategy: *reductio ad absurdum*. That phrase is the fancy Latin way to say "Proof by Contradiction." The technique is truly one of the most powerful tools mathematicians and logicians have up their sleeves.

I should warn you that the method sounds unusual and kooky at first. It takes some getting used to. To give you a sense of how this method works I'll use a relatively silly example: Marlene thinks her boyfriend, Sam, may have been the person to commit a robbery in her neighborhood. She corners him with that suspicion when they next meet. Sam replies, "Hey, suppose I really was the crook. Then would I have called the police, shown them that evidence, and then helped them search through the records? No way! That would be crazy! Therefore I can't be the crook. Don't worry."

Realistically Sam's logic is not airtight in this case, but what he is trying to do is use Proof by Contradiction to convince Marlene of his innocence. Let's look more closely at what Sam was doing. Generally speaking, Proof by Contradiction is used in situations where a straightforward proof would not work. Thus, we might conclude that Sam had no easy way to prove to Marlene that he is innocent (i.e., he had nothing like the Use a Diagram, Overload, or Row Compare methods that would help him in this specific situation). In the above case Sam may have thought that the only way to convince Marlene of his innocence was to show what would happen if one assumed that he was indeed guilty. Then he went on to demonstrate that the assumption that he is guilty leads to an absurdity (i.e., the guilty party helping out the police investigation). Sam's logic is not airtight, because it is possible that he helped the police to help them think he really is a good guy. It is unlikely, but possible.

In mathematics we sometimes use the same approach Sam did. If you can't prove what you want in a direct manner, assume the opposite of what you're trying to prove is true. Then using solid logic, show how that assumption leads to a contradiction.

Given this very general introduction to Proof by Contradiction, let's work through the rest of Game 20. At this point we know the following:

Correct colors: 1 Blue, 1 Green, 1 Orange

Incorrect colors: 2 Reds (there could be one), Yellow

Now let's suppose that you have a suspicion that one Red is a correct color (looking at Moves 1 and 2 indicates there's a decent probability that it is a correct color). Therefore, let's assume that Red is an *incorrect* color.

CONTINUED MASTERMIND REASONING FOR GAME 20

I've assumed Red is an incorrect color. Therefore I know from Move 1 that White must be a correct color. In addition I know from Move 3 that a second Blue must be a correct color. So now I know that Blue, Green, Orange, White, and a second Blue

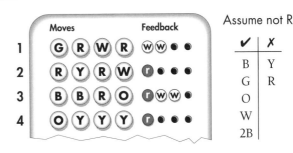

must all be correct colors. But I have 5 correct colors for only 4 positions! No way! Contradiction! Therefore, our assumption was incorrect. Red must be a correct color.

At this point we can deduce that the Mastercode includes Blue, Green, Orange, and Red thanks to Proof by Contradiction. Now it becomes much easier to solve the rest of the problem. Let's follow through with one possible way to think about solving the rest of the code.

FINAL MASTERMIND REASONING FOR GAME 20

I know now that Blue, Green, Orange, and Red are correct colors.

To find the positions I can start with the knowledge that Orange must go in Position 1 from the information on Move 4. Then I know, by looking at Move 2, that Red must go in Position 3 since Position 1 is already taken up by Orange. Next I know, by looking at Move 3, that Red in Position 3 is representing the red feedback peg. That means Blue cannot go in either Positions 1 or 2. Since Red is already in Position 3, then Blue must go in Position 4. This leaves the Green. Green must go in Position 2, the only open position left. Thus the code is: Orange, Green, Red, Blue.

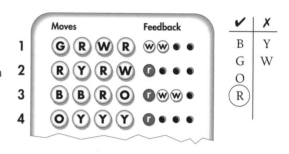

You may now have a deeper insight into the Latin term for this strategy: *reductio ad absurdum.* Or in everyday language: reduce to the absurd. When we use Proof by Contradiction, what we intend to do is to show that, based on a specific assumption, our reasoning leads to an absurdity. Since in a logical universe such absurdities are not tolerated, we know we have contradicted ourselves. This leaves only one culprit: the initial assumption. Therefore we conclude that the initial assumption must be incorrect.

When using Proof by Contradiction be very careful. It is an incredibly useful tool. Yet there is one major pitfall people run into when using this method. *The method only works if you come up with a contradiction.* Let's pretend that you make an assumption and the logical implications of that assumption don't lead to any contradiction. In that case the method tells you absolutely zip about the truth or falsehood of your assumption. "No contradiction" does not mean that the assumption is correct. Using this strategy, assumptions are conclusive only if they lead to an absurdity. Otherwise they remain simply assumptions—and assumptions are hardly solid evidence.

Perhaps the best way to understand the limitations of making assumptions that do not lead to contradictions is to look at an example. In the game situation below we can deduce some information without using Proof by Contradiction. Take a few minutes to explore this problem and deduce what colors need to be in the Mastercode.

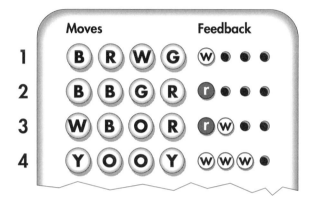

If you made a chart, it would probably look like the one below. That is, we can deduce from the information given that both Yellow and Orange need to be in the Mastercode while Green is out.

✔	✗
Y	G
O	

We know Yellow and Orange are in by applying the Overload Method to Move 4. We know Green is out by applying the Row Compare Method to Moves 1 and 3. However, we can't deduce any further information at this point. Looks like time for the all-powerful Proof by Contradiction method. By scanning the game situation it seems as if Blue might be part of the Mastercode. So, let us make the assumption that Blue is *not* in the Mastercode.

Take a few minutes to see whether you come up with a contradiction or not. As with a regular game situation, it is always useful to make a chart. Since we are using an assumption, we should make a separate chart and not add onto our original one which depicts only those colors we know *for sure* are in the Mastercode. It is also advisable to make something like a double-line to indicate which colors you knew about *before* making the assumption, and which findings are based on the assumption itself. When you have done as much as you can, read the reasoning given below.

MASTERMIND REASONING FOR GAME 21 (ASSUMING BLUE IS INCORRECT)

I've assumed Blue is an incorrect color. I know from Move 2 that Red must be a correct color since Blue and Green are incorrect. I know from Move 1 that White must be incorrect since Red is the one correct color in that Move. So, I know Orange, Yellow, and Red are in the Mastercode and either Orange or Yellow is used twice.

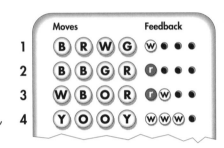

I know from Move 2 Red goes in Position 4. I know from Move 4 that Orange cannot go in Positions 2 or 3, and obviously can't go in Position 4. Thus Position 1 is the only place Orange can go. Therefore, from Move 4 the remaining slots of Positions 2 and 3 must be taken up by two Yellows.

What's happened? We made an assumption and did not come up with a contradiction. Instead, we came up with a viable solution: OYYR. Okay, now try assuming that Red is an incorrect color. Look at Game 21 and see if you come up with a contradiction. When you have made as much progress as you can, read the excerpt below.

MASTERMIND REASONING FOR GAME 21 (ASSUMING RED IS INCORRECT)

I've assumed Red is an incorrect color. I know from Move 2 that one and only one Blue must be a correct color since Red and Green are incorrect and there is only one feedback peg for two blue colors. I know from Move 1 that White must be incorrect since Blue is the one correct color in that move. So, Orange, Yellow, and Blue are in the Mastercode and either Orange or Yellow is used twice.

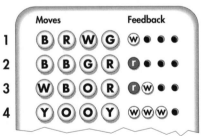

I know, by comparing the blue colors and feedback pegs in Moves 1 and 2, that Blue must go in Position 2 since it can't be correct in Position 1. I know from Move 4 that Yellow cannot go in Positions 1 or 4, and because of the position of the Blue it cannot go in Position 2. Therefore Yellow must go in Position 3. Orange is thus the only color that can go in both Positions 1 and 4. The Mastercode is: OBYO.

Once again we have made an assumption and did not come up with a contradiction. Instead, we came up with a viable solution: OBYO. We have now made two assumptions, neither of which led to a contradiction. Both, however, led to possible solutions.

What does all this mean? First, be very careful when using Proof by Contradiction. Assumptions that do not lead to contradictions do *not* themselves lead to solutions. Second, if there are two or more different possible Mastercodes based on different assumptions, then the game is unsolvable without another clue. Third, more often than not, when you're playing MASTERMIND you'll be looking at a game situation for which you cannot get the solution on the next move. Most of the games in this book can be solved in the next move if you skillfully use key problem-solving strategies. However, the examples and games in this book that cannot be solved in one more move are better examples of realistic MASTERMIND playing. Why is this important? Because even if you come up with two possible solutions to a game, what you have accomplished greatly reduces the number of possible Mastercodes. In the case of Game 21 it would make sense to play one of the possible Mastercodes. Thus, even if you don't come up with a contradiction, *reductio ad absurdum* is still a powerful technique for finding one of a handful of possible solutions.

The Varieties of Proof by Contradiction

There are three major categories of contradictions that will occur when Proof by Contradiction works. They are

◆ more colors than positions contradiction
◆ positions contradiction
◆ more (or fewer) feedback pegs than correct colors

In one example, Game 20, the contradiction occurred because we ended up concluding that there were more colors in the Mastercode than there were positions. However, this is not the specific way all instances of *reductio ad absurdum* work. Sometimes the contradiction occurs because the initial assumption leads you to conclude that Red (for example) must be in Position 1 but some other move indicates that Green must also be in Position 1. Since you can't have two colors in the same position, you have a contradiction. It is also common for the contradiction to occur because the initial assumption leads you to conclude that there are more correct colors than there are feedback pegs. For example, you may make an assumption that leads you to conclude that Red, Green, and Orange are all correct colors, but in Move 5 there are only two feedback pegs while all three colors show up in the move. Again you have a contradiction and must conclude that the initial assumption was incorrect.

A Challenging Game

Let's make sure of our approach to Proof by Contradiction by looking at one more example. This game is a bit trickier; we will need to use *reductio ad absurdum* more than once.

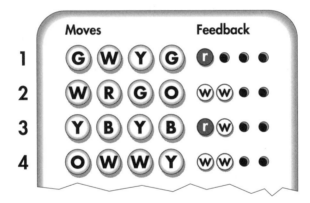

MASTERMIND GAME 22
6 COLORS, 4 POSITIONS

Given this game situation, our reasoning might appear as follows.

INITIAL MASTERMIND REASONING FOR GAME 22

Hmm, it doesn't seem that I can tell anything for sure! Okay, if I want to use Proof by Contradiction I should decide what type of information would be particularly useful to know. One of the difficult things about this game is that it is very hard to tell whether White or Yellow is a correct color—both are used a lot. I know from Move 1 that only one of those two colors can be correct. My hunch is that Yellow is a correct color. Therefore I'll assume the *opposite*: that Yellow is not a correct color.

You never know when *reductio ad absurdum* will be needed to solve a MASTERMIND game. Sometimes, as with Game 22, you seem to need it right from the start. At other times you need it in the middle or late stages of solving the Mastercode. Nonetheless, the general pattern of thinking displayed above is important.

Once you decide to try Proof by Contradiction, then you need to decide how to make your initial assumption. In general, look for which information holds the most *information potential*. Since White and Yellow appear often, it seems that knowing which of those two is correct is probably the best place to start in Game 22. You will not always make the right decision about what should be the initial assumption, but information potential is a useful guideline. In the case of Game 22 we could have as easily had a hunch that White was a correct color. One of those two assumptions will not lead to a contradiction. Let's now follow one way of reasoning about Game 22 employing Proof by Contradiction.

INTERMEDIATE MASTERMIND REASONING FOR GAME 22

I will assume that Yellow is an incorrect color. Then I know by Move 3 that there are two Blues in the Mastercode. Next I know, by looking at Move 4, that White has to be a correct color by the Overload Method (two Whites and an Orange with two feedback pegs). Great. That means from Move 1 that I now know that Green is incorrect. Hmm . . . now it's harder to tell anything more about the colors. Oh, but if I look at Moves 1 and 4, there's a contradiction! Move 1 tells me that White has to go in Position 2 but Move 4 tells me that White can't go in Position 2! That's a contradiction. Therefore, Yellow must be a correct color.

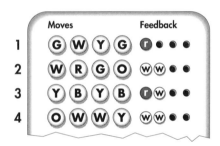

Assume not Y	
✔	✗
B	Y
2B	G
W	

This first *reductio ad absurdum* has helped us a little. But we still need some more crucial information. Let's follow one way to continue thinking about Game 22.

FINAL MASTERMIND REASONING FOR GAME 22

Okay, by knowing that Yellow is correct I can start to make some headway. First, I can tell from Move 1 that neither Green nor White is correct. Then I can tell from Move 2 that both Red and Orange have to be correct colors. Great.

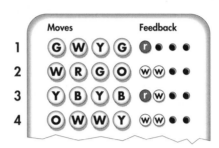

✔	✗
Y	G
R	W
O	

What I don't know now is whether Blue or a second Yellow is correct. My hunch is that Blue is in the code. Therefore I'll assume the opposite: that there is no Blue and that two Yellows are correct. Now if 2 Yellows are correct, I know from Move 1 that one Yellow must go in Position 3. Also, I can tell from Moves 2 and 4 that the Orange must go in either Position 2 or 3 since it can't go in Positions 1 or 4. But Yellow has already claimed Position 3. Therefore, Orange must go in Position 2.

Assume not B

✔	✗
Y	G
R	W
O	B
2Y	

This means the second Yellow must go in either Position 1 or 4. I can deduce from Move 4 that Yellow can't go in Position 4. Good. Oh, but in Move 3 the red feedback peg must stand for the Yellow in Position 3 and the white feedback peg must stand for the Yellow in Position 1. That means Yellow can't go in Position 1 either! That's not possible. This means that the second Yellow can't go anywhere since Positions 2 and 3 are claimed and it can't go in Positions 1 or 4. That's absurd. Therefore my assumption must have been wrong. Two Yellows can't be correct; there must be a Blue in the Mastercode. This means Yellow, Blue, Orange, and Red are the correct colors.

I hope finding out the positions is easier! Okay, from Move 1 (again!) I know that Yellow goes in Position 3. I also know from Moves 2 and 4 that Orange goes in Position 2. Then I can tell by looking at Move 3 that Blue can't go in Position 4. Therefore it must go in Position 1. Let's see, the only color left is Red and it must go in Position 4. So the Mastercode is: Blue, Orange, Yellow, Red.

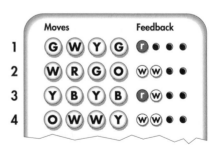

Game 22 used two Proofs by Contradiction. While this doesn't usually happen, it is possible. I think you can tell by now that there would be no way to solve the problem, and know you were absolutely correct, unless you had the *reductio ad absurdum* strategy up your sleeves.

Two Problems to Challenge You

To help you get used to this new technique, the following MASTERMIND games challenge you to use Proof by Contradiction using a given assumption. Your task is to find out if Proof by Contradiction works in each case; if it does, explain what the contradiction is that you found. The answers to the questions are given at the end of the chapter.

MASTERMIND GAME 23
6 COLORS, 4 POSITIONS

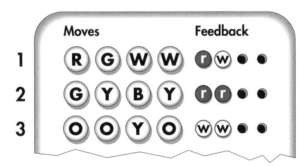

	First Challenge:	Assume that GREEN is incorrect.
		Do you come up with a contradiction? If so, what is it?
	Second Challenge:	Assume that YELLOW is incorrect.
		Do you come up with a contradiction? If so, what is it?
	Third Challenge:	Can you figure out the correct code?
		Do you need to use Proof by Contradiction any more times?

MASTERMIND GAME 24
6 COLORS, 4 POSITIONS

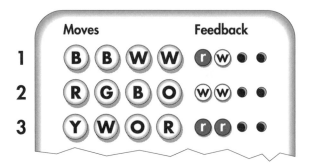

First Challenge: Assume that BLUE is incorrect.
Do you come up with a contradiction? If so, what is it?

Second Challenge: Can you figure out the correct code?
Do you need to use Proof by Contradiction any more times?

Two Last Problems with a Twist

Always keep in mind that at times you will use Proof by Contradiction and not come up with a contradiction. That's all right. You need to work on hunches about which colors you think are correct (or incorrect). Nonetheless, this is a very powerful method for obtaining solid information. If you learn to apply the method well, you will be able to solve problems that previously seemed impossible to solve.

Proof by Contradiction is a powerful technique in mathematics. A number of important proofs in geometry, algebra, and number theory (to just name three well-known fields) use Proof by Contradiction. If you are a Geometry or Advanced Algebra student, your teacher will be able to show you some proofs which utilize this powerful technique. Have fun with the problems below. Most of them, but not necessarily all of them, need Proof by Contradiction to solve the game.

There is a twist to these problems. Instead of using 6 colors and 4 positions, these games use 6 colors and 5 positions! These are not games you could play on your regular MASTERMIND board. Instead, they are more difficult games that generalize beyond the board game. By now you may be accustomed to solving MASTERMIND games using paper and pencil. These games will seem a little harder but perhaps not so unusual.

Hints (at three levels) are provided at the end of the chapter, as are the answers for the games. Make sure to give each game your best effort before looking up a hint or

the answer. Work through the reasoning yourself so you fully understand the hint/
answer. Good luck!

MASTERMIND GAME 25
6 COLORS, 5 POSITIONS

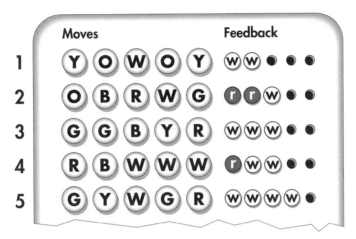

MASTERMIND GAME 26
6 COLORS, 5 POSITIONS

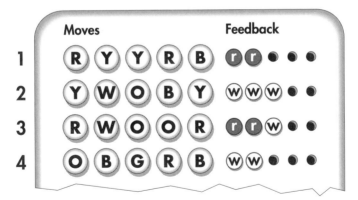

MASTERMIND ANSWERS FOR GAMES 23 AND 24

Note: With all of the hints and reasoning given below, keep in mind that the reasoning and diagrams represent one way to illustrate the situation. There may be other paths that arrive at the same solution.

Game 23

First Challenge: Assume GREEN is incorrect.

Yes, you should come up with a contradiction. Here's why. Given our assumption, we can come up with the following diagram:

Assume not G

✔	✗
W	G
Y	
O	
B or 2Y	
R or 2W	

This diagram tells us that our contradiction has to do with having more colors (5) than positions (4).

Second Challenge: Assume YELLOW is incorrect.

Yes, you should come up with a contradiction. You can actually find the contradiction in a number of ways in this case. Here's one way. We can come up with the following diagram:

Assume not Y

✔	✗
O	Y
2O	
G	
B	
R or W	

So the contradiction has to do with having more colors (5) than positions (4).

Another way to find a contradiction is to notice from Move 3 that two Oranges must be in the Mastercode, but all the Oranges have white feedback pegs. Since there are three Oranges in that move, that means two Oranges have to go in Position 3! A contradiction, once again.

Third Challenge: Can you figure out the correct code? *Reductio ad absurdum* needed?

Yes, you can figure out the correct code, and you don't need to use *reductio ad absurdum* again.

Game 24

First Challenge: Assume BLUE is incorrect.

No, you do not come up with a contradiction. You can come up with the following diagram based on the assumption that Blue is incorrect:

Assume not B

✔	✗
W	B
2W	

Notice that you do not end up with too many colors. Nor do you find any contradictions about their positions. Since there is no contradiction, there is nothing that we can say conclusively. We don't know that Blue is incorrect for sure. It may be either correct or incorrect at this point.

Second Challenge: Can you figure out the correct code? *Reductio ad absurdum* needed?

No, you cannot figure out the correct code. Not enough information is present.

LEVEL-ONE HINTS

Game 23   Assume Green is incorrect.

Game 24   not solvable

Game 25   Assume Yellow is incorrect. You'll find a contradiction in Move 3 after some preliminary deducing.

Game 26   Assume Orange is incorrect. You'll find a contradiction (after some work) based on the feedback in Move 2.

LEVEL-TWO HINTS

Game 23   Assume Yellow is incorrect.

Game 24   not solvable

Game 25   Assume Red is incorrect. Again, after some preliminary deducing, you'll find a contradiction in Move 5.

Game 26   Assume Red is incorrect. You'll find a contradiction based on having 6 colors for 5 positions.

LEVEL-THREE HINTS

Game 23   Start figuring out positioning even if you don't have all of the colors yet. A combination of positioning information with color information will allow you to find that White has to be in the Mastercode and in which position.

Game 24   not solvable

Game 25   Positioning can be tricky. Find that Yellow has to go in Position 3 first before doing the other positioning.

Game 26   Yellow is in the Mastercode by an Overload in Move 2. Positioning can be tricky, but find position for Red and then Orange. The rest will follow.

ANSWERS

Game 23   G Y O W

Game 24   not solvable

Game 25   W R Y W G

Game 26   R Y W O W

CHAPTER 6

Becoming a Master Player

Through the first five chapters of this book you have learned about seven discrete problem-solving skills. They are techniques that you have used to solve a variety of game situations. Those seven skills include:

◆ Establish subgoals
◆ Make a chart
◆ Use deductive thinking
◆ Eliminate possibilities
◆ Overload Method
◆ Row Compare Method
◆ Proof by Contradiction

So far you've used these strategies to deduce information from given moves. Most of those games could be solved in one more move. But in a real MASTERMIND game, you're not given preselected moves. You have to choose what moves to make yourself. Will these strategies actually help you do that? You bet. This chapter provides a short introduction to how you might use these strategies while playing. Before you read on, you might want to try playing a few games and experimenting yourself with different ways to apply the strategies you've learned. Then you can come back to the book and read some suggestions for initial moves, intermediate moves, and final moves in a simulated MASTERMIND game.

Prepare Thyself for the Game!

You always want to be proactive when playing MASTERMIND. Four of our strategies can be "primed" before you even start playing: (a) using deductive logic, (b) making a chart, (c) establishing subgoals, and (d) eliminating possibilities. While there is always a small element of luck in playing MASTERMIND, you want to plan on using solid deductive logic to solve the Mastercode as efficiently as possible. Be ready to think clearly.

The strategy of making a chart allows you to reduce the cognitive energy your brain puts into trying to remember colors. Instead, you can channel that energy into a more focused approach to playing the game. Some people make a chart by using paper and pencil (as we have done in this book) but others find it more useful to make a physical chart. You can do this by creating a pile of the six possible colors used in the Mastercode. This is the "unknown" pile since you don't know the status of the colors yet. When you discover a particular color is in the Mastercode, put that color peg in a separate "in" pile. Likewise, when you discover that a particular color is "out," put that color peg in a third pile for the "out" colors. As you can see, this is simply a physical representation of the paper-and-pencil charts that you created. Use whichever method works best for you.

Third, establishing subgoals will help you focus on critical outcomes without becoming overwhelmed. Too many players start out wanting to solve for color and position at the same time. For example, let's say you know from a first move that Red has to be in the Mastercode. Some players will then waste the next couple of moves trying to figure out which position Red has to go in. Although the feedback pegs *may* give you critical information about positions that you can use very early in the game, don't worry too much about positioning until you have figured out all or most of the colors in the Mastercode.

Fourth, remember that it is just as useful to eliminate possibilities as it is to find correct colors and positions. Don't be disappointed if you receive no feedback pegs for a move. A "no feedback" move with multiple colors gives you a great deal of useful information! Eliminating colors also helps you determine when multiples of the same color are in the Mastercode. For example, if you have eliminated four colors, then you know the Mastercode has to be comprised of some combination of the two colors left.

Now that you're prepared, let's work through a simulated game as if we were playing it, one move at a time, and we'll see how some of the other strategies can be applied.

The First Moves

What is a good initial move? There may be several, but to increase your probability of finding information it is useful to keep the Overload Method in mind. How can you try to force an overload? Recall that to have an overload you need multiple uses of one color and enough feedback pegs to deduce that at least one of the colors must be in the Mastercode. Imagine you made the move below. How might it help you?

If you get no feedback pegs, you'll eliminate both Yellow and Red. If you get one feedback peg, you'll at least know that either Yellow or Red is in the Mastercode (but you won't know which). If you get two or more feedback pegs, you'll have an overload: at least one of those pegs will be for Yellow. So whatever happens, this move will give you useful information. Let's see what the feedback is:

The move helps a lot. From this move, and the feedback, you know that Yellow has to be in the Mastercode. In addition, you know either a second Yellow or a Red has to be in the Mastercode. Thus, from the very first move you are able to conclude some bit of the Mastercode for certain.

What can we gather from this example? Although it won't always result in certainty, you increase your probability of getting solid information by taking advantage of a potential overload situation. Thus, if you want to play only two colors in the first move, this logic suggests you play three pegs of one color and one peg of the second color in order to maximize the probability that you will create an overload situation.

Notice that if you use four different colors you have a situation in which there is no possibility of creating an overload. Thus while it may be attractive to use four colors, generally you will garner more useful information using a two-color opening. Of course, if you use only one color with four pegs, then you will necessarily have an overload if you receive any feedback pegs at all. And if you receive no feedback pegs, you'll eliminate that color. But while using one color at a time is effective in terms of certainty, it also usually requires taking many more moves to find the Mastercode than using the two-color opening. While it is possible to create overload situations using three different color pegs (two of one color, one each of two other colors), this type of move generally leads to many fewer actual overloads. Thus the two-color opening is suggested as the best way to "force" an overload situation.

If you use a two-color opening, you'll probably want to use a similar strategy for your next two moves until you have used up all six possible colors in the Mastercode. There are exceptions to this, of course. For example, if you get four feedback pegs with the first two moves, you can stop trying for overloads and start working on positions. If a two-color move yields only one feedback peg (and thus no overload), you might want to move to a different strategy to narrow your information. Let's try another two-color move and see if we can force another overload.

We're hoping for two or more feedback pegs so that we'd know Orange was in the Mastercode. No feedback pegs would help a lot, too: we could eliminate Orange and White. Let's see what we get.

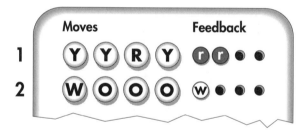

One feedback peg. That's bad luck—the least information we could get. Oh well. At least we know that either White or Orange is in the Mastercode.

The Intermediate Moves

After the initial moves, what should you do? One way to proceed is to make another two-color move using Blue and Green, which haven't been used yet. Another option, however, is to try to create a Row Compare situation. Let's try that. Move 3 below uses exactly the same color combination as Move 2 *except* that a Green is used instead of a White peg.

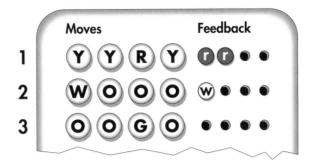

So what good does this do us? Let's imagine the possibilities. Imagine you receive no feedback pegs. In that case you now know that neither Orange nor Green are in the Mastercode, and that White has to be in the Mastercode. On the other hand, imagine you receive two feedback pegs. In that case you would know Orange has to be in the Mastercode (due to an Overload), that Green has to be in the Mastercode (due to a Row Compare), and that White is not in the Mastercode (again due to a Row Compare). Notice that you cannot get either 3 or 4 feedback pegs with this move because of the feedback in Move 1. The last case is that of receiving one feedback peg. Although you can't tell anything for certain with one feedback peg, you still gain critical information. If there is one feedback peg, you know *either* there is one Orange and neither White nor Green in the Mastercode *or* you know there is both White and Green in the Mastercode while Orange is out.

Let's see what we get.

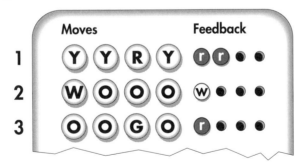

Tough luck again: only one feedback peg. What can you figure out from these first three moves? Actually, you can tell quite a bit. First, either Green or Orange is correct in Move 3. IF Green is correct, then Red cannot be (because they'd have to occupy the same position due to the red feedback pegs), nor could Orange be in the Mastercode. In addition, White would have to be correct as well as two Yellows from Move 1. Thus the colors in the Mastercode would have to be: Green, White, Yellow,

Yellow. On the other hand, IF Orange is correct in Move 3, then Green and White cannot be in the Mastercode. In addition, Orange would have to go in Position 1 (can you tell why?). We still would not know which colors from Move 1 are correct. And it is likely that we have another color, Blue, in the Mastercode or there is a multiple of Red (can you tell why?). Thus, after the third move we can drastically reduce the possibilities for Mastercodes.

Do you see how valuable Row Compare can be in the example given? No matter what the feedback is, you have gained critical information that will help you solve the Mastercode. Keep in mind the Row Compare Method. It can be a very helpful tool as you start making intermediate moves. We have enough information to start trying some final move strategies.

As a fourth move we might use a combination of the information we have garnered from earlier moves but without using any of our specific strategies. Note that we know Yellow is in the Mastercode, but we don't know in which position. It would also be useful to know whether Orange is in the Mastercode or not. Finally, we don't know anything about Blue at this point. All of these factors may lead you to make a move such as that illustrated in Move 4 below:

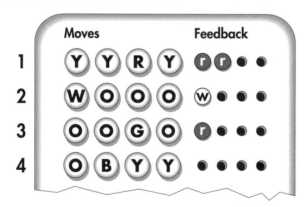

Would such a move be useful? Most likely yes. If you receive one feedback peg, you know that there cannot be a second Yellow, a Blue, or an Orange. These conclusions, in turn, would eliminate other possibilities. If you receive two or more feedback pegs, the information you can deduce may be more ambiguous. However, given all of the information from the previous moves, it is likely that you can combine the information from all four moves to deduce quite a bit after this move. Were there other moves we could have made at this point? Yes. But the general approach was to make a move which combined ambiguities from previous moves and existent unknowns (such as whether Blue was in the Mastercode or not). Typically after three or four moves there are a variety of good moves one can make as long as you take advantage of the unknown factors from more than one of the previous moves.

Final Moves

Notice that we're starting to say "if" a lot as we analyze our moves. That's an indication that we're ready to try some assumptions. Once you have gathered enough information through your first 3–5 moves, you can often (though not always) take advantage of Proof by Contradiction. The simplest way to use it is as a checking device. If there are a small number of possible code combinations, assume one code combination is true. If you come up with a contradiction then you can eliminate it! On the other hand, if there is no contradiction then you have to consider that particular combination as a *possible* Mastercode. Remember, however, that when we have no contradiction this does not mean we have found the answer!

Let's get back to our game and see what the feedback was:

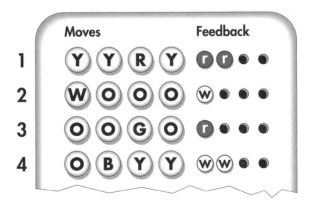

So we got two white feedback pegs. What should you play next? When trying out possible next moves we may want to take advantage of Proof by Contradiction *before* we make our move. Recall that at this point we know that: (a) at least one Yellow has to be in the Mastercode. From the fourth move we can reduce our possibilities to one of three scenarios: (a) two Yellows are in the Mastercode, (b) a Yellow and a Blue are in the Mastercode, or (c) a Yellow and an Orange are in the Mastercode. Which one of these three possibilities is it? Let's see if any of these possibilities leads to a contradiction.

First, let's assume that Orange is a correct color. Given that assumption you can relatively quickly come up with the following chart and positioning:

$$
\begin{array}{c|c}
\checkmark & \times \\
\hline
\text{\textcircled{Y}} & \text{B} \\
\text{O} & \text{W} \\
\text{R} & \text{G}
\end{array}
$$

However, there is a problem with this scenario. From Move 4 we know that Orange cannot go in Position 1, but from Move 2 we know that Orange cannot go in any of the other Positions either! Therefore our assumption that Orange is a correct color has led to a contradiction! Good, now we can eliminate Orange.

The second possibility is that Blue is the correct color. Given that assumption you can come up with the following chart:

$$
\begin{array}{c|c}
\checkmark & \times \\
\hline
\text{\textcircled{Y}} & \text{O} \\
\text{B} & \\
\text{R} & \\
\text{W} & \\
\text{G} &
\end{array}
$$

As you can see, the problem is that we now have five correct colors for only four positions. A contradiction again! So now we can eliminate Blue as a possible color.

Notice that we have eliminated the first two possibilities, and that leaves only the assumption of two Yellows. By the "eliminate possibilities" strategy we know two Yellows have to be in the Mastercode. However, it is only by chance that we chose to check out the two Yellows possibility last. For practice you may want to check out the two Yellows assumption to make sure you do not come up with a contradiction.

Based on these first four moves you can deduce what the Mastercode must be. Try to determine the Mastercode for yourself. The answer is given at the end of the chapter.

Final Suggestions

There is no surefire way of solving each and every game. However, by taking advantage of the skills you have learned in this book you will find that you can often solve MASTERMIND games in 6 moves or less—even under the worst circumstances. Remember to be prepared: think deductively, focus on the initial subgoal of finding the color combination, make a chart, and eliminate possibilities. During your initial moves, increase your chances of getting helpful information by creating potential overload situations. During your intermediate moves help yourself by creating potential Row Compare situations. Finally, during the final moves in a game you can greatly help yourself by using Proof by Contradiction to make sure whether a potential move can be a Mastercode (or not).

Use your skills wisely. You will find yourself becoming a master player soon. And you will likely find that many of the strategies you have learned will help you to think more clearly and efficiently in other topics covered in your mathematics class.

(Psst . . . the Mastercode is: YYGW.)

CHAPTER 7

Informal Proofs

In most areas of life it is important not only to come up with good ideas or solutions, but also to have the ability to clearly *communicate* those ideas and solutions to others. This general principle also holds in mathematics. A *proof* is a way of communicating why a mathematical result has to be as it is. This and the next chapter serve as an introduction to mathematical proofs, only you'll apply proof techniques to MASTERMIND games. In general we can say that the standard for a good proof is that it is convincing. When you do a proof, the form of communication needs to be convincing in a way that clearly shows how you were thinking about a problem and what set of logical steps you took in solving the problem.

Good communication is important because it allows you to convince another person that your way of thinking about a problem was sound. However, developing good communication skills in mathematics is not the same as using communication skills in politics or everyday life. In mathematics the emphasis is on logical clarity.

Perhaps the best way to understand the need for proofs is to try one out for yourself. Do the exercise on the next page. After completing the exercise, compare your answer with those created by other students in your class.

Warm-up Exercise for Mathematical Proofs

Pretend you have a good friend who lives many miles away and cannot be reached by telephone. They challenge you to solve a MASTERMIND game. If you simply send them the written answer, they will hardly be convinced. Your friend will want you to *show* that you knew how to reason out the problem instead of just making a lucky guess. First, solve the game given below. Then write out your explanation of how you knew the answer has to be as you solved it.

MASTERMIND GAME 1
6 COLORS, 4 POSITIONS

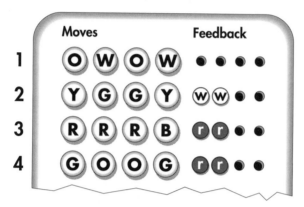

To share some common mathematical language, let's agree to refer to the moves by their number (such as Move 3). Let's also refer to the positions the colors are in by Position 1, 2, 3, 4, or 5 (if there are five positions). Position 1 will be the position on the far left. Position 4 (or 5) will be the position on the far right.

An example of how one person wrote up a proof to Game 1 is given on the following two pages. Don't look until you have tried writing a proof for yourself!

FINDING THE MASTERCODE IN GAME 1

I started by looking at Move 1. Since there were no feedback pegs in that move, I knew that neither Orange nor White could be in the Mastercode. Then I looked at Move 4. Since we know Orange is not correct, and since there are two red feedback pegs, then there must be two Greens in the Mastercode. In addition, because the feedback pegs were both red, I know Green must be correct in both Position 1 and Position 4.

Next I looked at Move 3, which also has two red feedback pegs. I already know Greens occupy Positions 1 and 4. Since Move 3 has no Green color pegs, then the colors in Positions 2 and 3 must be correct. In this case both positions are filled by Red.

Thus, the Mastercode has to be: GRRG.

Note some of the language used in the example proof: moves, positions, Mastercode, since, because, must, then, and thus. You probably used some of the same words. You may have proven the Mastercode using a different series of steps though (there often is more than one way to show what the Mastercode has to be). One of the keys of a proof is that in the end you demonstrate to someone else what the answer <u>must be</u>! However, even if you communicated your proof differently, somehow you had to be able to direct the reader to specific parts of the problem by telling the reader exactly what peg or combination of pegs you were talking about.

There are three positive components that all persuasive proofs are likely to include: (1) the reader knew where to look, (2) the reader was given each key conclusion of the person's thinking (e.g., "White has to go in Position 2"), and (3) the reader was given the reasoning by which the writer was able to deduce each conclusion. In short, even a good paragraph-formatted proof has to be well-organized in order to be effective.

There are clear disadvantages of using a paragraph format to write a proof. It's somewhat easy for the reader to get lost. It's not always clear when we have left one step of reasoning and are about to begin another. And, finally, it's difficult to read lots of writing when you only want very specific information. Mathematicians are concerned with writing proofs that are extremely clear. This means it needs to be easy for the reader to follow the "flow" of the logical argument, the steps of reasoning need to be clearly indicated, and the focus should be on substance, with as little clutter as possible. A mathematical proof, therefore, looks more like a table or chart than it looks like a short story or essay.

Proof for
MASTERMIND Game
Vol. I

Proof for
MASTERMIND Game
Vol. III

The type of proof you wrote out above is usually referred to as an informal proof. This means the proof contains sound logical reasoning but is not expressed in traditional mathematical style. The next step in writing a proof, which will still be informal, is to give more supporting structure.

To help you think about writing a more coherent and easy-to-read informal proof, a structure is suggested below. You may decide to alter this structure on your own—that's fine, but first try it out. Keep in mind that no matter what structure you use, the three key components of effective mathematical communication need to be there: (1) where to look, (2) what's the conclusion, and (3) what's the reasoning.

INFORMAL PROOF STRUCTURE	
WHERE TO LOOK	**REASONING AND CONCLUSION**
1. Move 3	<u>Since</u> there are no feedback pegs, <u>then</u> Red and White are not correct colors.
2. Move 2	<u>Since</u> we know Red and White are not correct colors by Step 1, <u>then</u> there is one and only one Blue in the Mastercode.

Note that there are two columns ("Where to Look" and "Reasoning and Conclusion"). Further note that each step of reasoning is numbered and can later be referred to as "Step x." In the Reasoning and Conclusion column the reasoning is given first (with each part of the reasoning prefaced by an underlined logic word such as <u>since</u>) followed by an underlined <u>then</u>, which precedes the conclusion of the reasoning. This type of structure makes it much easier for a reader to navigate through your logical argument. Try it out on MASTERMIND Game 1 (shown earlier in this chapter). Talk about your results in class. The following page provides one example of how the proof, written in this format, might look.

INFORMAL PROOF OF MASTERMIND GAME 27

WHERE TO LOOK	REASONING AND CONCLUSION
1. Move 1	<u>Since</u> there are no feedback pegs, <u>then</u> neither Orange nor White are correct colors.
2. Move 4	<u>Since</u> Orange is not correct (Step 1), and <u>since</u> there are two red feedback pegs, <u>then</u> there are two Greens in the Mastercode and they go in Positions 1 and 4.
3. Move 3	<u>Since</u> there are 2 red feedback pegs and <u>since</u> Positions 1 and 4 are already taken by Greens (Step 2), <u>then</u> there are two Reds in the Mastercode in Positions 2 and 3.
4.	<u>Therefore,</u> the Mastercode is GRRG (Steps 2 & 3).

6 colors, 4 positions

Moves	Feedback
1 O W O W	● ● ● ●
2 Y G G Y	ⓦⓦ ● ●
3 R R R B	ⓡⓡ ● ●
4 G O O G	ⓡⓡ ● ●

We will develop the sophistication of our proofs as we progress in this book. However, it is hard enough for most people to get the hang of writing their own proofs in a simple manner. It takes practice to get good at writing informal proofs in mathematics. Do you see how laying out the informal proofs in a very organized fashion helps the reader (and sometimes you) to better understand how you are thinking? One strategy for writing mathematical proofs is the "Create Subgoals" strategy you learned earlier. In essence this approach divides the proof into a series of smaller problems. On one level you first try to prove all the colors in the Mastercode and then try to prove their positions. At a more detailed level, each step of a proof is the solution to a smaller problem (e.g., that White has to be in the Mastercode). Many MASTERMIND proofs involve the use of 8 to 14 steps (or solutions to small problems that help to solve the big problem).

On the following pages you are given four MASTERMIND problems. You have seen each one before. Your challenge is to solve them again, but also to be aware of *how* you solved them. Not surprisingly your second challenge then is to write an informal proof for each of these problems (an example proof for each problem is given later in the chapter). Compare your proofs with the ones included in this book. Keep in mind that there is usually more than one way to develop a proof. What you need to evaluate is whether or not each line of reasoning is solid, justified, and complete. Good luck.

Solve and Prove!

MASTERMIND GAME 2
6 COLORS, 4 POSITIONS

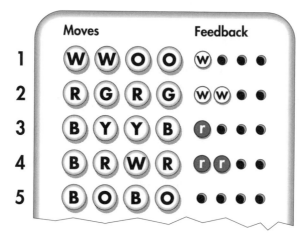

MASTERMIND GAME 3
6 COLORS, 4 POSITIONS

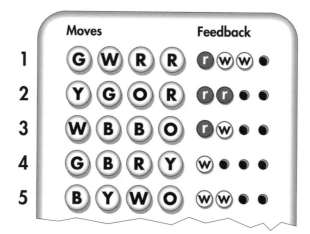

MASTERMIND GAME 18
6 COLORS, 4 POSITIONS

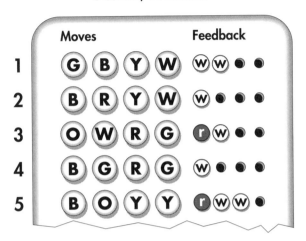

	Moves	Feedback
1	G B Y W	w w ● ●
2	B R Y W	w ● ● ●
3	O W R G	r w ● ●
4	B G R G	w ● ● ●
5	B O Y Y	r w w ●

MASTERMIND GAME 20
6 COLORS, 4 POSITIONS

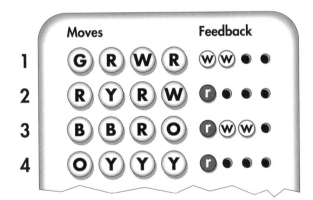

	Moves	Feedback
1	G R W R	w w ● ●
2	R Y R W	r ● ● ●
3	B B R O	r w w ●
4	O Y Y Y	r ● ● ●

INFORMAL PROOF OF MASTERMIND GAME 2

WHERE TO LOOK	REASONING AND CONCLUSION
1. Move 5	<u>Since</u> there are no feedback pegs, <u>then</u> neither Blue nor Orange is a correct color.
2. Move 1	<u>Since</u> Orange is not correct (Step 1), and <u>since</u> there is one feedback peg, <u>then</u> there is one and only one White in the Mastercode.
3. Move 3	<u>Since</u> Blue is not correct (Step 1), and <u>since</u> there is one feedback peg, <u>then</u> there is one and only one Yellow in the Mastercode.
4. Move 4	<u>Since</u> Blue is not correct (Step 1) and <u>since</u> White is correct (Step 2) and <u>since</u> there are two feedback pegs, <u>then</u> there is one and only one Red in the Mastercode.
5. Move 2	<u>Since</u> one and only one Red is correct (Step 4) and <u>since</u> there are two feedback pegs, <u>then</u> there is one and only one Green in the Mastercode.
6.	<u>Therefore</u> the correct colors are White (Step 2), Yellow (Step 3), Red (Step 4), and Green (Step 5).
7. Move 4	<u>Since</u> White is in the code (Step 2) and <u>since</u> the feedback peg for it is red, <u>then</u> White must go in Position 3.
8. Move 3	<u>Since</u> there's one red feedback peg and <u>since</u> there is one Yellow in the Mastercode (Step 3), <u>then</u> <u>either</u> the Yellow in Position 2 is correct <u>or</u> the Yellow in Position 3 is correct. But White is in Position 3 (Step 7). <u>Therefore</u>, Yellow has to go in Position 2.
9. Move 4	<u>Since</u> one Red is in the code (Step 4), <u>then</u> one of the red feedback pegs refers to <u>either</u> the Red in Position 2 <u>or</u> the Red in Position 4. But Yellow is in Position 2 (Step 8). <u>Therefore</u>, Red has to go in Position 4.
10.	<u>Since</u> Green is in the code (Step 5), and <u>since</u> Positions 2, 3, and 4 are taken by colors Yellow, White, and Red, respectively (Steps 8, 7, and 9), <u>then</u> Green has to go in Position 1.
11.	<u>Therefore</u>, the Mastercode is GYWR (Steps 10, 8, 7, 9).

6 colors, 4 positions

Moves	Feedback
1 W W O O	w • • •
2 R G R G	w w • •
3 B Y Y B	r • • •
4 B R W R	r r • •
5 B O B O	• • • •

INFORMAL PROOF OF MASTERMIND GAME 3

WHERE TO LOOK	REASONING AND CONCLUSION
1. Move 1	<u>Since</u> there are 3 feedback pegs and 2 Reds, <u>then</u> there is a Red in the Mastercode (Overload Method).
2. Move 4	<u>Since</u> there is only 1 feedback peg and <u>since</u> by Step 1 we know Red is a correct color, <u>then</u> Green, Blue, and Yellow must all be incorrect colors.
3. Move 1	<u>Since</u> Green is not a correct color (Step 2) and <u>since</u> there are 3 feedback pegs, <u>then</u> there are 2 Reds and 1 White in the Mastercode.
4. Move 3	<u>Since</u> Blue is not a correct color (Step 2) and <u>since</u> there are 2 feedback pegs, <u>then</u> there is an Orange in the Mastercode.
5.	<u>Therefore</u> the correct colors are Red (Step 1), White (Step 3), Red (Step 3), Orange (Step 4).
6. Move 2	<u>Since</u> both Orange and Red are in the Mastercode (Step 5) and <u>since</u> both feedback pegs are red, <u>then</u> Orange must go in Position 3 and Red in Position 4.
7. Move 3	<u>Since</u> Orange goes in Position 3 (Step 6), <u>then</u> the one red feedback peg must represent the White. <u>Therefore</u>, White goes in Position 1.
8.	<u>Since</u> Steps 5, 6, and 7 dictate that there is only one free position left, <u>then</u> the second Red must go in Position 2.
9.	<u>Therefore</u> the Mastercode is WROR (Steps 5–8).

6 colors, 4 positions

INFORMAL PROOF OF MASTERMIND GAME 18

WHERE TO LOOK	REASONING AND CONCLUSION
1. Move 5	<u>Since</u> there are 3 feedback pegs, <u>then</u> at least one of the 2 Yellows is in the Mastercode (Overload Method).
2. Move 2	<u>Since</u> Yellow is a correct color (Step 1) and <u>since</u> there is only one feedback peg, <u>then</u> Blue, Red, and White must not be in the Mastercode.
3. Move 3	<u>Since</u> there are two feedback pegs and <u>since</u> Red and White are not in the Mastercode (Step 2), <u>then</u> Orange and Green must be in the Mastercode.
4. Move 5	<u>Since</u> there is no Blue in the Mastercode (Step 2) and <u>since</u> there are 3 feedback pegs, <u>then</u> two Yellows are in the Mastercode.
5.	<u>Therefore</u> the correct colors are Yellow (Step 1), Orange (Step 3), Green (Step 3), and Yellow (Step 4).
6. Move 4	<u>Since</u> Green is in the Mastercode (Step 3) and <u>since</u> there is a white feedback peg, <u>then</u> Green cannot go in Positions 2 or 4.
7. Move 3	<u>Since</u> Green cannot go in Position 4 (Step 6) and <u>since</u> the 1 white feedback peg must represent the Green in Position 4, <u>then</u> Orange must go in Position 1. <u>Therefore</u> Green has to go in Position 3, and the two Yellows go in the remaining positions.
8.	<u>Therefore</u> the Mastercode is OYGY (Steps 5–7).

6 colors, 4 positions

	Moves				Feedback			
1	G	B	Y	W	w	w	•	•
2	B	R	Y	W	w	•	•	•
3	O	W	R	G	r	w	•	•
4	B	G	R	G	w	•	•	•
5	B	O	Y	Y	r	w	w	•

INFORMAL PROOF OF MASTERMIND GAME 20

WHERE TO LOOK	REASONING AND CONCLUSION
1. Move 3	<u>Since</u> there are 3 feedback pegs and 2 Blue color pegs, <u>then</u> there is a Blue in the Mastercode (Overload Method).
2. Moves 1 & 2	<u>Since</u> White, Red, and Red are common to Move 1 and Move 2 and <u>since</u> there is an additional feedback peg in Move 1, <u>then</u> there is a Green in the Mastercode and Yellow is not in the Mastercode (Row Compare Method).
3. Move 4	<u>Since</u> Yellow is not a correct color (Step 2) and <u>since</u> there is one red feedback peg, <u>then</u> Orange must be in the Mastercode and Orange must go in Position 1.
4. Move 2	<u>Since</u> we cannot tell whether Red or White is the correct color in Move 2, <u>then</u> we will use Proof by Contradiction. <u>Assume</u> Red is incorrect. <u>Then</u> Blue, Blue, and Orange must be correct colors from Move 3. Also, <u>then</u> Green and White must be correct colors from Move 1. <u>Contradiction</u> because we now have 5 colors for 4 positions! <u>Therefore</u> Red must be a correct color.
5.	<u>Therefore</u> the correct colors are Blue (Step 1), Green (Step 2), Orange (Step 3), and Red (Step 4).
6. Move 2	<u>Since</u> Red has to go in either Position 1 or 3 <u>because</u> of the one red feedback peg, and <u>since</u> Orange goes in Position 1 (Step 3), <u>then</u> Red must go in Position 3.
7. Move 3	<u>Since</u> Red goes in Position 3 (Step 6), <u>then</u> the white feedback pegs indicate Blue cannot go in Positions 1 or 2. <u>Therefore</u> Blue can only go in Position 4.
8.	<u>Since</u> Steps 3, 6, and 7 dictate where Orange, Red, and Blue must go, <u>then</u> remaining color Green must go in Position 2.
9.	<u>Therefore</u> the Mastercode is OGRB (Steps 3, 6, 7, and 8).

6 colors, 4 positions

	Moves				Feedback			
1	G	R	W	R	w	w	•	•
2	R	Y	R	W	r	•	•	•
3	B	B	R	O	r	w	w	•
4	O	Y	Y	Y	r	•	•	•

Hopefully the exercises you have done gave you some further insight into how to write a mathematical proof. To enhance your abilities you could practice writing proofs for any of the previously played games in this book. Many people find it significantly harder to write a proof than to solve a problem. That is not surprising given that many people find it harder to clearly communicate something rather than just doing it. The informal proofs in this chapter were written in everyday English, although in a fairly structured manner. You will find few mathematical proofs written in this form, however. The next chapter will develop a symbolic language for communication. The advantage of writing in symbolic language is both its mathematical power and its elegance. That is, the brevity of symbols often allows a person to say more in a briefer, clearer fashion.

CHAPTER 8

Formal Proofs

In the last chapter you were introduced to the need for mathematical communication. You wrote some informal proofs that would convince another person with your logical line of thinking. As you are already aware, few mathematical proofs look like the ones presented in the previous chapter. In formal mathematical proofs we are accustomed to seeing things like mathematical symbols as well as axioms and theorems. There are good reasons each of these things is included in a mathematical proof, but the end result can look quite daunting at first.

In this chapter you will learn how to write formal mathematical proofs for the game of MASTERMIND that are fairly similar to standard symbolic logic proofs. And they're structured in a two-column proof format used in many geometry textbooks. This chapter represents only a beginning. To become proficient you will need more practice outside of this book.

Mathematical Symbols

Mathematicians are always in search of brevity. One problem with everyday language is that we use a lot of words that aren't essential to the meaning we are trying to convey. Consider this phrase, "Oh my gosh, I can't believe Whitney Houston made another number one song! What an amazing feat!" A mathematician might boil down the essence of the above quotation to something like: Houston = great. It's shorter, it easily highlights the main point someone is trying to make, and it's effective (i.e., other mathematicians know exactly what you are trying to say).

In this chapter we are going to re-look at the four informal proofs we did in the previous chapter. We are going to transform them into formal MASTERMIND proofs. To do this, however, we need to develop a mathematical symbol language for the MASTERMIND game. For example, in mathematics and logic the symbol ∴ is used to stand for "therefore," which is a commonly used word in many mathematical proofs. I present one set of mathematical symbols that could be used in writing formal MASTERMIND proofs. Some of these symbols are commonly used in a similar way in many areas of mathematics. Other symbols are quite specific to the game of MASTERMIND.

One MASTERMIND Symbol Language

Symbol	Meaning
→	implies (or "then")
∧	and
∨	or
∴	therefore
1f	1 feedback peg (color not relevant)
1r1w	1 red feedback peg and 1 white (color <u>is</u> relevant)
G	Green is in the Mastercode
~G	Green is <u>not</u> in the Mastercode
① G	1 and only 1 Green is in the Mastercode
G = P1	Green is in Position 1
G ≠ P2	Green is <u>not</u> in Position 2
[2]	from Step 2
GGRR ≡ Mcode	GGRR equals the Mastercode

The symbols presented above are quite useful for explaining all of the key occurrences in MASTERMIND proofs. For example, we can refer to colors which are in the Mastercode but for which we don't know the correct position (e.g., "Yellow is a color in the Mastercode" is expressed simply as "Y"), as contrasted with a statement for a sequence of colors which we know makes up the Mastercode, or is equal to the answer set, such as "WRYG ≡ Mcode."

Writing Formal Proofs

Try writing the four proofs from the games used in the previous chapter with your new mathematical symbol language. The following pages present a likely way to write each of the four proofs using symbols.

There are many things you may notice about writing formal proofs. At first it may seem harder and less intuitive to do. While this may be true, writing such proofs becomes "intuitive" with practice. In addition you may notice that formal proofs are shorter, making it easier to find information than it is in an informal proof. It becomes easier to follow the "guts" of a mathematical argument. On the other hand, formal proofs assume that you will fill in some of the explicit explanations that are left out of the symbolic language. They assume you can piece together all the relevant information as long as you are told exactly where to look.

Try writing a proof for Game 1 from Chapter 7. Then compare your proof to the example symbolic proof below.

Example Formal Proof

FORMAL PROOF OF MASTERMIND GAME 1

WHERE TO LOOK	REASONING AND CONCLUSION
1. M1	$Of \rightarrow \sim O \wedge \sim W$
2. M4	$\sim O \wedge 2r \rightarrow G = P1 \wedge G = P4$
3. M3	$2r \wedge G = P1 \wedge G = P4 \rightarrow R = P2 \wedge R = P3$
4.	$\therefore GRRG \equiv Mcode$

6 colors, 4 positions

	Moves	Feedback
1	O W O W	● ● ● ●
2	Y G G Y	ⓦⓦ ● ●
3	R R R B	ⓡⓡ ● ●
4	G O O G	ⓡⓡ ● ●

Now try formal proofs of Games 2, 3, 18, and 20 from Chapter 7. Example formal proofs of these games appear on the following pages.

MASTERMIND GAME 2
6 COLORS, 4 POSITIONS

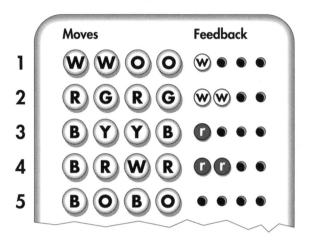

MASTERMIND GAME 3
6 COLORS, 4 POSITIONS

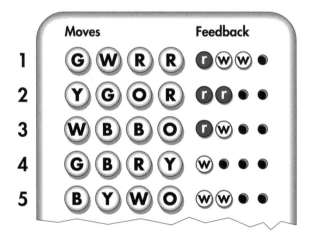

MASTERMIND GAME 18
6 COLORS, 4 POSITIONS

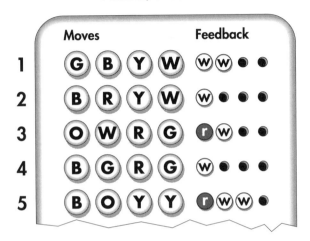

MASTERMIND GAME 20
6 COLORS, 4 POSITIONS

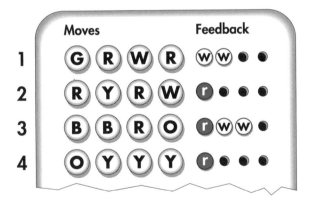

FORMAL PROOF OF MASTERMIND GAME 2

WHERE TO LOOK	REASONING AND CONCLUSION
1. M5	$0f \rightarrow \sim O \wedge \sim B$
2. M1	$\sim O \wedge 1f \rightarrow ①W$
3. M3	$\sim B \wedge 1f \rightarrow ①Y$
4. M4	$\sim B \wedge W \wedge 2f \rightarrow ①R$
5. M2	$①R \wedge 2f \rightarrow ①G$
6.	$\therefore$ W, Y, R, G
7. M4	$W \wedge 2r \rightarrow W = P3$
8. M3	$1r \wedge ①Y \rightarrow Y = P2 \vee Y = P3.\ W = P3 \rightarrow Y\ P3.\ \therefore Y = P2$
9. M4	$①R \wedge 2r \rightarrow R = P2 \vee R = P4.\ Y = P2 \rightarrow R\ P2.\ \therefore R = P4$
10.	$①G \wedge Y = P2 \wedge W = P3 \wedge R = P4 \rightarrow G = P1$
11.	$\therefore$ GYWR $\equiv$ Mcode

6 colors, 4 positions

	Moves	Feedback
1	W W O O	ⓦ ● ● ●
2	R G R G	ⓦⓦ ● ●
3	B Y Y B	ⓡ ● ● ●
4	B R W R	ⓡⓡ ● ●
5	B O B O	● ● ● ●

FORMAL PROOF OF MASTERMIND GAME 3

WHERE TO LOOK	REASONING AND CONCLUSION
1. M1	$3f \rightarrow R.$ Overload Method.
2. M4	$1f \wedge R \rightarrow \sim G \wedge\ \sim B \wedge \sim Y$
3. M1	$\sim G \wedge 3f \rightarrow W \wedge 2R$
4. M3	$\sim B \wedge 2f \rightarrow O$
5.	$\therefore$ R, W, R, O
6. M2	$O \wedge R \wedge 2r \rightarrow O = P3 \wedge R = P4$
7. M3	$O = P3 \rightarrow 1r$ for W. $\therefore W = P1$
8.	$[5] \wedge [6] \wedge [7] \rightarrow R = P2$
9.	$\therefore$ WROR $\equiv$ Mcode

6 colors, 4 positions

	Moves	Feedback
1	G W R R	ⓡⓦⓦ ●
2	Y G O R	ⓡⓡ ● ●
3	W B B O	ⓡⓦ ● ●
4	G B R Y	ⓦ ● ● ●
5	B Y W O	ⓦⓦ ● ●

FORMAL PROOF OF MASTERMIND GAME 18

WHERE TO LOOK	REASONING AND CONCLUSION
1. M5	$3f \wedge 2Y \rightarrow Y$. Overload Method.
2. M2	$Y \wedge 1f \rightarrow {\sim}B \wedge {\sim}R \wedge {\sim}W$
3. M3	$2f \wedge {\sim}R \wedge {\sim}W \rightarrow O \wedge G$
4. M5	${\sim}B \wedge 3f \rightarrow 2Y$
5.	$\therefore$ O, G, Y, Y in Mcode
6. M4	$G \wedge 1w \rightarrow G$ P2 $\wedge$ G P4
7. M3	$[5] \wedge G$ P4 $\wedge 1r \rightarrow O = P1$
8. M3	$[6] \,\&\, [7] \rightarrow G = P3 \wedge Y = P2 \wedge Y = P4$
9.	$\therefore$ OYGY $\equiv$ Mcode

6 colors, 4 positions

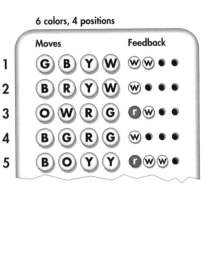

	Moves	Feedback
1	G B Y W	w w ● ●
2	B R Y W	w ● ● ●
3	O W R G	r w ● ●
4	B G R G	w ● ● ●
5	B O Y Y	r w w ●

FORMAL PROOF OF MASTERMIND GAME 20

WHERE TO LOOK		REASONING AND CONCLUSION
1.	M3	$3f \rightarrow B$. Overload Method.
2.	M1 ∧ M2	2f in M1∧ 1f in M2 $\rightarrow G \wedge \sim Y$. Row Compare Method.
3.	M4	$\sim Y \wedge 1r \rightarrow O = P1$
4.	M2	$\sim Y \rightarrow R \vee W$. Proof by Contradiction: Assume $\sim R$. $\sim R \rightarrow B \wedge 2B \wedge O$ in M3. Also $\sim R \rightarrow G \wedge W$ in M1. 5 colors for 4 positions. Contradiction! ∴ R.
5.		∴ B, G, O, R in Mcode
6.	M2	$1r \rightarrow R = P1 \vee R = P3$. $O = P1$ [3] $\rightarrow R = P3$
7.	M3	$R = P3 \rightarrow B$ P1 ∧ B P2. ∴ B = P4
8.		$[3] \wedge [6] \wedge [7] \rightarrow G = P2$
9.		∴ OGRB ≡ Mcode

6 colors, 4 positions

	Moves				Feedback
1	G	R	W	R	W W • •
2	R	Y	R	W	r • • •
3	B	B	R	O	r w w •
4	O	Y	Y	Y	r • • •

Elegance in Formal Proofs

Mathematicians often refer to some proofs as being "elegant," which is usually shorthand for saying the proof is written in either a very simple or a very powerful manner. As you become more skilled in mathematical communication, you may want to think about the elegance of mathematical proofs. A proof may be considered elegant if it takes advantage of a clever insight. All elegant proofs, however, are relatively short.

There is usually more than one way to prove a specific Mastercode. These different ways are fine. But among these possibilities, mathematicians usually refer to the proof done in the fewest number of steps (given that the reasoning was correct and clear) as the most elegant proof. Sometimes a proof is shorter because someone saw a way to take fewer steps in the solution. Other times the proof is shorter because someone used a very powerful technique (such as Proof by Contradiction) to create a shorter solution path. On the other hand, if you try to make a proof shorter by simply cramming several steps into one, you sacrifice clarity and, therefore, elegance.

MASTERMIND Mathematics: Logic, Strategies, and Proofs • ©1999 Key Curriculum Press

When sharing proofs in a class, it may be useful to think about the notion of elegance. In this way you can critically appraise and appreciate a variety of proofs that are all valid but may differ in their structural simplicity or the power of the techniques used to write them. A mathematical proof expressed succinctly and convincingly can appear so simple that many more people can follow its line of reasoning than with a longer, more complicated proof. Simple, succinct, and convincing presentation of reasoning equals elegance in mathematics.

Advanced Topic: Axioms and Theorems

Whenever you are working with a mathematical system (algebra or geometry, for example), there are always properties of those systems that are referred to as axioms and theorems. The same is true for the mathematical system of MASTERMIND. In general terms, axioms are features of a logical system that are so fundamental and obvious that it is easy for everyone to accept those features as being true without any formal proof. Furthermore, it is important for a set of axioms to be consistent; that is, they should not contradict one another. Both the issues of obviousness and consistency have a long and fascinating history in mathematics. In reality these two issues are subtle and sometimes hard to understand. For example, what's obvious to one person may not be obvious to another. However, the reason for having axioms at all is that it is never possible to prove *everything* within a mathematical system. Axioms are those few statements about a system that we will not try to prove but will simply accept as true. As an "Axiom" exercise, try the following before reading further:

Exercise

Think about the game of MASTERMIND. Then think about what features of the game are so basic that everyone will easily accept them as being true. Make sure that your axioms are inclusive (i.e., no important features of the game are left out) but not overly long.

After talking about the conclusions made in your group or class, compare them against the suggested MASTERMIND axioms listed below. Were your axioms inclusive? Did you have too many? Would you change the axioms listed below? If so, how and why?

Suggested MASTERMIND Axioms:

Axiom 1 In each hole there is one and only one color peg.

Axiom 2 Each color peg has one and only one color.

Axiom 3 Each feedback peg refers to one and only one color peg.

Axiom 4 During one turn, the codebreaker uses exactly as many color pegs as there are positions in the Mastercode.

Axiom 5 Every red feedback peg denotes a correct color in the correct position. Every white feedback peg denotes a correct color in an incorrect position.

Axiom 6 For any game there is one and only one Mastercode.

Axiom 7 In any one game, the codemaker and the codebreaker need to agree on the number of color pegs in the Mastercode before playing.

Some people may object to the above axioms in that they seem identical to the rules of the game. Their observation is correct, but there's no reason to object. In any mathematical system the axioms in essence constitute the "rules of the game" of that particular system. Axioms serve as those features of the system that we can count on and that define how we "play" within that system.

Every statement in a mathematical system that can be proved is called a theorem. Thus, a complete system is made up of axioms and theorems. New theorems are "proven" by using logic, the authority of the axioms, and previously established theorems. Each of the game results we proved in earlier chapters could now constitute theorems within our MASTERMIND system. In fact, if you wanted to take the time, you could tackle the more general (and harder) proof of showing that something like the Overload Method or Row Compare Method is valid within the MASTERMIND system! However, these more difficult proofs should not be tackled until you have worked through this chapter.

Finally, in any proof situation you are usually presented with a set of facts that are accepted as true. These are usually referred to as the "givens" for a particular problem. Givens include statements such as "line 1 is parallel to line 2," "ABCD is an equilateral quadrilateral," and so on. In MASTERMIND the givens are the specific plays of the game. From our axioms and our givens, we go on to prove a particular result. Thus whenever you are shown a game situation, you are also being presented the "givens" for a particular proof.

A mathematician may object to calling the results of our MASTERMIND proofs theorems. The point they would make is that our theorems are "weak." Theorems that are *significant* are theorems which make general statements. The more situations a theorem can apply to, the more powerful it will be considered. The "theorems" in this chapter only apply to a particular set of circumstances. On the other hand, if we could prove a theorem like "Every time there is only one of each color in the Mastercode, the game will not need more than five plays to find the Mastercode," we would then have a theorem which provides us with information useful in many different situations. As a rule of thumb, the more powerful the theorem, the harder it is to prove. Of course once you have proved it, you have a powerful tool to use in the future. Thus, if you proved the Overload Method you would be proving a general, strong theorem.

Summing Up

A critical aspect of mathematical thinking is developing the ability to communicate mathematically. This process of mathematical communication, through the use of proofs, may seem exotic and strange to you at first. Yet with adequate practice and discussion within the classroom, you will have the knowledge and skill to write proofs in algebra, geometry, and many other areas of mathematics. It is important to keep in mind that the purpose of mathematical communication is to help others know exactly how you are thinking. In this regard, proofs that are simple, succinct, and convincing end up being more effective (or "elegant") in reaching the ultimate goal of clear mathematical communication.

CHAPTER 9

The MASTERMIND Olympics

Contained in this chapter are nine *really* hard games. Some of the especially challenging games may well take you 60 minutes or more to solve each one. Adults have tried in vain to solve some of these problems! However, they are all solvable. Hints and answers are provided as in earlier chapters. Nonetheless you are highly encouraged *not* to use this help unless absolutely necessary. Learning is greatly enhanced when you work as hard as you can in solving these problems. By now you should *know* if your answers are correct.

Use Abstraction to Feel That Burn!

The first step in mathematics is to squarely look at a situation and determine what is its essential makeup. The mathematician will then work with that "core" and leave the "fluff" behind. For instance, when a mathematician is figuring out the volume of liquid a water tank can hold, she or he is not concerned with the color of the tank, or its location, or any number of everyday factors which may apply to that particular water tank. The mathematician is simply looking at certain core conditions of the situation—in particular, the radius and height of the tank. The "fluff" about the water tank—its color, location, age, etc.—may be important in the everyday world, but the mathematician is only

Go get a scoop —then we'll start measuring.

concerned with the relationships between the key measurable properties of the tank. This ability to determine the logical core of a situation, separate it from the fluff, and then continue to work with only that core describes the process of *abstraction*.

Abstraction also allows us to generalize. For example, in a very concrete way if we want to determine the volume of one particular water tank, we could endeavor to scoop out the water and count how many cubic units of water are in the tank. Or we can use abstraction to observe the key mathematical characteristics of the tank— namely, its height and radius—to determine its volume. We can then go on to measure the height and radius (instead of the tiresome scooping of water) and then calculate the volume of the water tank. This second procedure shows a greater level of abstraction. However, we can even further abstract that calculation into an all-purpose formula (using the symbols r and h) that can be used to calculate the volume of *any* cylinder. The formulaic version is so powerful that we can apply it to a hypothetical cylinder drawn on a piece of paper, such as an architect or contractor might do, to determine how large a water tank would be needed to meet the needs of a whole community. In this way abstraction allows us to generalize beyond a specific situation into an all-purpose formula or strategy that can be used in a wide variety of circumstances. In fact, this process of abstraction leading to generalization is what gives mathematics much of its power.

The bottom line is this: In order to do any really useful mathematics you need to be able to abstract. That is, you need to be able to put the "essence" of an action, procedure, or thing into symbolic form. By abstraction we can tackle types of MASTERMIND games that we could never dream of solving before. You've already had a small introduction to abstraction in the exploration of Proof by Contradiction (Chapter 5), where the last two problems used six colors and *five* positions. By abstracting we can not only play MASTERMIND using pencil and paper, but also extend (or generalize) the MASTERMIND rules beyond the physical limitations of the game board and pegs.

We could generalize from the basic MASTERMIND game in many ways. In this chapter we have chosen to make the games significantly harder by creating game situations which use *eight* colors and *five* positions. Thus there are both more colors and more positions than you are accustomed to using on the MASTERMIND board. How much harder are these games? The regular MASTERMIND game has 6^4 or 1,296 possible solutions—and your challenge was to find the particular Mastercode the codemaker had created. In this chapter's super MASTERMIND games, you have 8^5 or 32,768 possible solutions!

You are given two game situations below. Each one comes complete with hints and solutions at the end of the chapter. Use your thinking cap as well as you can to get a feel for this new expanded version of MASTERMIND. The two new colors are purple (or P) and turquoise (or T). Good luck.

MASTERMIND GAME 27
8 COLORS, 5 POSITIONS

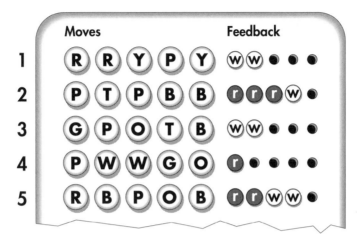

MASTERMIND GAME 28
8 COLORS, 5 POSITIONS

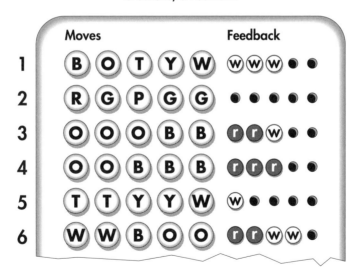

The Final Seven: Enter Only If Logically Brave

Now that you've had a little practice with this generalized version of MASTER-MIND, let's go on to the "MASTERMIND Olympics." In the following pages you will find seven top-notch games. Hints and answers have been provided for these games. In the end, however, what should convince you (as a teacher or as a student) is the worthiness of someone's proof (informal or formal) of the solution. In this way you will be responding like a good mathematician.

With these problems it may turn out that a combination of mini-proofs from different students helps to create one mega-proof that convinces everyone of the answer. Thus, one student may be able to show why Red has to be in the Mastercode, while another student is able to show why Green and White *cannot* be in the Mastercode. A final proof can be woven together from such mini-proofs. It is the clarity of logical reasoning that should convince the reader that a specific color or position, or the Mastercode itself, is correct.

Perhaps most importantly, these problems are so hard that students can learn a great deal from working on them as a class or cooperatively in small groups. You may not be able to solve these problems working individually—but when 25–40 students marshal their thinking power together, they will often be able to collectively solve the problem. Thus these problems can provide a very tangible experience showing how difficult problems can be solved in teams: very few, if any, individuals would solve the problem on their own. Certainly this type of cooperative experience is typical in mathematics and the sciences where a number of different people will contribute novel and important thinking over a number of years before the problem is completely solved.

These final problems are probably the most reflective of actual mathematical practice in another way. Mathematicians often take large chunks of time to solve interesting problems. Solving interesting problems that may take 40–60 minutes is a step towards the level of persistence needed in more realistic mathematical activity. It is advisable that after solving the problem you then write a proof. In this way you may find the games both challenging and highly rewarding since you have had the opportunity to engage in the full circle of mathematical activity: understanding the problem, exercising logical reasoning to solve the problem, spotting significant patterns that may help unlock the code, and finally communicating your findings to others in a convincing manner.

Best of luck with the problems that follow!

MASTERMIND GAME 29
8 COLORS, 5 POSITIONS

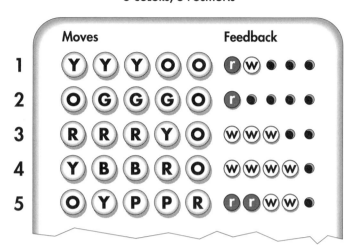

MASTERMIND GAME 30
8 COLORS, 5 POSITIONS

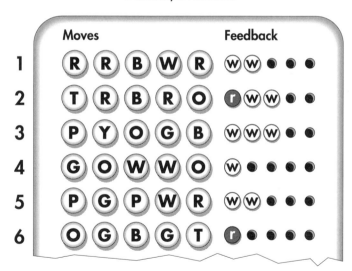

MASTERMIND GAME 31
8 COLORS, 5 POSITIONS

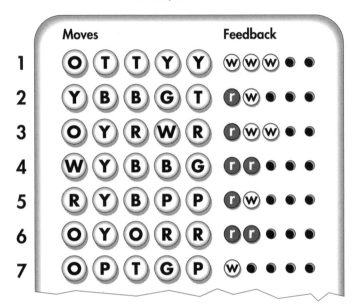

MASTERMIND GAME 32
8 COLORS, 5 POSITIONS

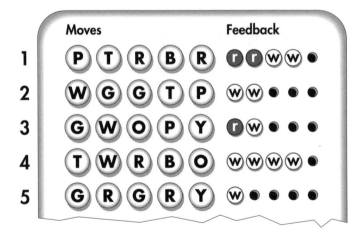

MASTERMIND GAME 33
8 COLORS, 5 POSITIONS

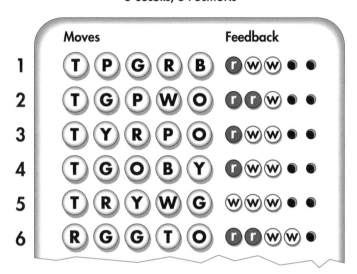

Note: The last two games use *nine* colors and five positions. The ninth color is represented by the letter X.

MASTERMIND GAME 34
9 COLORS, 5 POSITIONS

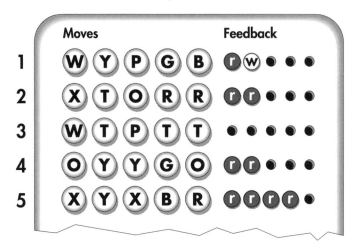

MASTERMIND GAME 35
9 COLORS, 5 POSITIONS

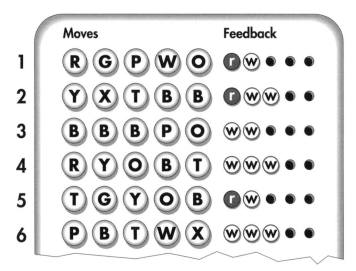

     MASTERMIND Mathematics: Logic, Strategies, and Proofs • ©1999 Key Curriculum Press

LEVEL-ONE HINTS

Note: For all of the games it is best to make a chart!

Game 27 Use Overload Method twice in Move 2.

Game 28 Use Overload Method twice in Move 6 and once in Move 4.

Game 29 Overload in Moves 3, 4, and 5.

Game 30 Assume not Red.

Game 31 Assume not Yellow.

Game 32 There is an Overload in Move 1. From Move 5 you can then tell that there is only one Red. This then enables you to deduce other things. Alternatively, you can use various Proofs by Contradiction. But if you do, you should be aware that this becomes a very, very tricky game. In all it involves the use of six Proofs by Contradiction. Start off by assuming not Orange.

Game 33 Also difficult, involving five Proofs by Contradiction. First assume Orange incorrect.

Game 34 Again, many contradictions to pursue. First assume not Red. The contradiction comes not with too many colors, but rather due to the positioning of the deduced colors based on this assumption. It's a very nice and advanced use of Proof by Contradiction.

Game 35 First assume that Blue is incorrect. Then Row Compare with Moves 4 and 5.

LEVEL-TWO HINTS

Game 27   Moves 3 and 4 allow you to eliminate lots of colors.

Game 28   Moves 1 and 4 tell you there can't be two Oranges.

Game 29   Assume not Green.

Game 30   Row Compare with Moves 3 and 6. This is a very tricky and nonstandard use of Row Compare as Move 6 has one feedback peg and Move 3 has three feedback pegs. You can actually determine two colors which have to be in and one color that has to be out using this unusual Row Compare. A great example of a more generalized use of this method.

Game 31   Row Compare with Moves 3 and 6.

Game 32   Next two contradictions work by assuming Turquoise is incorrect, followed by assuming Blue is incorrect. (These hints are useful if you take the Proof by Contradiction route to solving this problem; otherwise, be aware that White is not in the Mastercode due to Move 2 and previous colors that are known to be in, or out of, the Mastercode.)

Game 33   Assume Red incorrect, then assume two Greens correct (or Turquoise incorrect). The second suggested Proof by Contradiction is very interesting in that it involves "nested" Proofs by Contradiction in which there is essentially a mini-proof within the larger Proof by Contradiction. Hopefully you'll understand this when you try the particular assumption of two Greens correct.

Game 34   Assume not Yellow.

Game 35   Assume that two Blues are <u>correct</u>. This is different from typical applications where we assume a color wrong. We already know there is one Blue in the Mastercode, but knowing there cannot be two Blues will be quite helpful. Again you will find the contradiction in the positioning phase.

LEVEL-THREE HINTS

Game 27   From Move 2 you can tell a few positions using position knowledge gleaned from Moves 3 and 4.

Game 28   Positioning of Orange: look at Moves 1 and 4. Then deduce where Orange cannot go. Find position of Blue next. Move 6 will then give position of White.

Game 29   Find positions. Easiest to find position of Orange first.

Game 30   The next step after the Row Compare is to see that Orange has to be in the Mastercode. The rest is pretty straightforward.

Game 31   Overload Method works given you already know that Orange is out of the Mastercode in Move 1.

Game 32   Now come three contradictions involving positioning. First assume Red in Position 1, then Purple in Position 1, then Orange in Position 3.

Game 33   Since Turquoise is not correct, Move 2 gives quite a bit of help with regard to positions.

Game 34   Assume not Blue.

Game 35   This is the very tricky move in this game: Row Compare Moves 2 and 5. Keep in mind that you already know certain things, such as Green is incorrect and a second Blue is incorrect. This is another advanced form of Row Compare which takes pattern-seeking strategies to a new level. The conclusion will be that X has to be in the Mastercode while Orange is out.

ANSWERS

Game 27   P B P B R

Game 28   O W B W B

Game 29   O P Y B R

Game 30   O P R R Y

Game 31   W Y Y R T

Game 32   O T B P R

Game 33   O G T R O

Game 34   X Y Y B R

Game 35   X R P Y B